PAY NOW, DIE LATER

PAY NOW,

Random House
New York

DIE LATER

What's Wrong with Life Insurance:
A Report on Our Biggest and
Most Wasteful Industry •

by James Gollin

THIRD PRINTING

© *Copyright, 1966, by James Gollin*

All rights reserved under International and Pan American Copyright Conventions. Published in New York by Random House, Inc., and simultaneously in Toronto, Canada, by Random House of Canada Limited.

Library of Congress Catalog Card Number: 66–12013

Manufactured in the United States of America

DESIGNED BY JAIME DAVIDOVICH

For Jane

Introduction

ONE MONDAY late in January of 1966 two gentlemen dropped in on Random House, the publishers of this book. One of these visitors was the senior vice-president of a major life insurance company in New York. The other held high office in one of the many insurance-industry trade associations. Their errand had a simple enough purpose. They said they had heard a lot about *Pay Now, Die Later*. (Indeed they had. Months earlier I had thoroughly discussed my plans for the book with these same officials.) Both men said in effect that a book like this one might cause a great deal of harm. The people at Random House could help, they added, by letting the two of them inspect the book's galleys before publication.

Being the kind of publisher that respects both its authors' rights and its own integrity, Random House turned down their request.

In the course of further conversation, these executives indicated they would see to it that *Pay Now, Die Later* was kept out of the hands of as many life insurance agents as possible. Finally the two officials departed, having failed either to satisfy their curiosity about the book's contents or to intimidate Random House with this threat to its sales efforts. The odds are that neither of them had the least idea of the impression they left behind.

INTRODUCTION

After you've read a few chapters of this book, I think you'll understand why I begin with the incident at Random House. Certainly the blundering of these two nervous executives isn't the issue here. But like too many others in their business, they behaved as if the American life insurance industry was full of important secrets that should be kept hidden. This episode only underscores the need for a book about the industry these men are so anxious to protect.

I think that they and their industry do have much to hide, much to be ashamed of and embarrassed by. Certain habits and practices of the life insurance business are outrages that ought to be stopped. Although this book is by no means just a catalogue of wrongdoings, I have tried to make plain what I think is wrong, not with a few unethical insurance men or a few companies but with the entire industry.

Most of my evidence comes from within the industry itself. The statistics, for example, are drawn from official life insurance publications available to anyone for the asking. Many factual references come from standard references like *The World Almanac* or from *The New York Times*. But more often I have used material (confidential surveys and reports, speeches, company publications, and the like) not normally accessible to the public, though familiar to hundreds of people in the life insurance business.

I've deliberately refrained from pointing an accusatory finger at any given company, person, or concept, preferring to name names when praise is due. By the same token, this book is no sales pitch for my own pet theories about insurance. I don't believe, for instance, that one form of life insurance is better than all others. I'm not touting mutual funds, the stock market, or any other rival (real or imagined) of the insurance industry. Nor does the book "prove" that life insurance is a swindle, a gigantic fraud. If life insurance is a fraud, then 120,000,000 of us—not to mention the entire national economy—are co-conspirators along with the biggest industry in this country.

To me, it's much more intriguing to suggest that life insurance and the strange industry which supplies it are both integral parts of the American Dream. In short, life insurance is a cherished version of the material richness and total blissful security that so many of us prize above all else. Yet like other subdivisions of the American Dream, this one has flaws, the most crucial being that no dream of security can or should pass as substitute for the real thing. Therefore, I think we need to wake up to what we do every time we buy life insurance, to probe the reality behind this vast enterprise that we have revered for so long.

Many people have helped me with this book. For their very different kinds of encouragement, advice, and patience, I am grateful to my agent, Lynn Nesbit, and to James H. Silberman and Margaret Harrell of Random House. Above all, his sensitive editorial surgery and unstinting personal support entitle Robin Jones to much of the credit (but none of the blame) for the way the book has gradually taken shape.

Throughout the life insurance industry, people have given me their time, their interest, and the benefit of their hard-won knowledge. Dozens of executives and specialists in many different companies have spoken freely in exchange for my promise not to reveal their identities. I hope that each of them will recognize himself, but I'm sure that nobody will be able to recognize his fellow informants. In due course, the reader will meet those others who are (by permission) quoted directly. I must also mention with thanks the several hundred life insurance agents (and ex-agents) whose stories, ideas, and comments have salted my research.

INTRODUCTION

And my own customers as well as many other insurance owners have lent willing and important co-operation.

Finally, I'd like to thank Timothy and Douglas, who have given up to this book so many hours that rightfully belonged to them.

Contents

CONTENTS

PAY NOW, DIE LATER

"Good evening, Mr. Doe."

—*the Agent*

1 . *You Only Know What the Salesman Tells You*

THE AMERICAN LIFE INSURANCE INDUSTRY is the biggest business in the world, and life insurance itself is one of our society's most remarkable and universal institutions. Almost none of us can escape being exposed to insurance. This industry's tireless efforts to make us buy more and more insurance have long since become part of our folklore. In the words of the old jingle, "Nobody has endurance like the man who sells insurance"—except, perhaps, the patient public that buys it.

But most Americans know little about their own life insurance and almost nothing about the industry that provides it.

In part this lack of knowledge stems from the life insurance industry's determination to keep secret its methods and practices, to operate as much as possible behind tightly closed doors. And the industry's traditional mistrust of the public and underestimation of our intelligence only perpetuates our ignorance and confusion.

But there's another reason why people understand very

little about life insurance and the life insurance industry.
We don't want to know. Because Americans have some
rather strange ideas and some curious uncertainties about
life, death, and money, our society has nurtured this vast
institution which we like to believe can prolong life, abolish
death, and even make us rich. In return, all we have to do
—or desire to do—is pay money, co-operate, and not be too
inquisitive. And so, today Americans insure their lives for
three quarters of a *trillion* dollars—a sum equal to one and
one seventh times the total national income. Yet at the same
time, the mechanics of the system whereby we obtain this
insurance remain, to most of us, a riddle wrapped in a
mystery inside an enigma.

With the industry surrounded by silence and the public
caught up in such uneasy reticence, the entire subject of life
insurance and its place in American society has become
something to keep quiet about. Even so, within that society
the life insurance industry is almost as ubiquitous as death
itself. Life insurance is a business whose yearly income has
now reached $30,000,000,000, whose assets of $150,000,-
000,000 exceed the total national wealth of Spain, Austria,
Greece, and all the Scandinavian countries combined. And
the very fact of its vast size and scope has convinced the
industry that the public should remain unenlightened about
life insurance and unaware of how this business really does
operate. In short, the industry openly argues that as long as
it functions effectively, it owes the public no explanations.
In an open society no institution should dare to make, and
no citizen should countenance, such an assumption. That
is the major premise of this book.

So the chapters that follow will scrutinize this massive
enterprise from many different angles and in a harsher light
than the rosy glow in which the industry prefers to be seen.

Part of this book's purpose is to draw an accurate portrait, to explain the workings of this mysterious but enormously powerful business empire. Another part of that purpose is to probe those strange—but peculiarly American—attitudes which have led us to enshrine life insurance as a national institution. This in turn involves probing into other patterns of commercial motives and public needs in order to discover what makes life insurance tick. But most important, we shall also be uncovering, step by step, what the functioning of this industry means to every single one of us who owns, or who may need, life insurance.

One theme will recur again and again: communications. For many reasons, the life insurance industry has long chosen to conduct its affairs in a strange jargon, a kind of Mandarin, that mystifies and alienates everybody who has to cope with it. In fact, more than one life insurance company has sought the aid of "communications consultants" to remedy the problem of making itself understood. (For instance, the Prudential retains Dr. Rudolf Flesch, author of *Why Johnny Can't Read,* as its expert on communications.) But the muddle and mystification still seem to grow, reaching an unfortunate peak for the customer just when he needs clarity and precision the most.

Therefore, one of the great services a book like this can render is to translate life insurance into English. To eliminate the language barrier, key insurance concepts will be presented in plain language. This often means drawing distinctions between such concepts and the dozens of clichés and merchandising formulas that the industry accepts as the right way to explain its products. Once this impenetrable terminology is stripped away, you may be surprised to find that the basic life insurance ideas possess a kind of spare, austere elegance. You'll also see why most people, although they may be veteran life insurance buyers, find it hard to figure out precisely what they own.

Muddled language aside, the other reason for this general lack of knowledge about insurance is that most of us only know what a salesman tells us. That's why this inquiry into life insurance begins with a hypothetical sales situation. By analyzing the familiar ritual of an insurance sale, we'll quickly discover that dispassionate, factual information about the product is the *last* thing an insurance salesman uses to sell that product. We'll see in detail what the artful salesman substitutes for an informative approach to insurance. As a result, you yourself may begin to realize that a straightforward explanation could be helpful indeed. Ultimately this book will focus on such an explanation.

So for the moment let's suppose you're a man aged thirty-five, married, with two children, working in the upper-middle-management reaches of a major corporation. You own your own home and a car, and you like to go sailing. Let's also assume that you're happily married, that your youngsters are getting along well in grade school, and that your company considers you a man on the way up.

One day at the office you get a telephone call. The carefully modulated voice at the other end of the line greets you and introduces its owner as a life insurance salesman. Somehow (and in a later chapter on marketing we'll find out exactly how) this gentleman has gotten hold of your name and discovered where you work. Now, after a moment or two of affable conversation, he suggests that it might be a good idea if the two of you could get together. Perhaps the best place would be at your home, where, in the salesman's words, "there won't be so many interruptions." You half-heartedly make an appointment, which in the press of business you promptly forget. On the evening of the appointment you're watching television and unwinding with a highball when the doorbell rings and you suddenly remember that it's the insurance man.

You agreed to this interview *not* because you had any intention of buying more life insurance—your G.I. insurance, your company's group plan, and a $10,000 policy you bought some years ago seem like enough. But somewhere at the back of your mind are a few questions about your present life insurance. These the salesman promised with alacrity to cover if you'd see him.

As you answer the doorbell, the life insurance man is standing on the front step, briefcase in hand. He's dressed much the way you dress for business; he wears a hat (hats are *de rigueur* in his trade); and you notice that he seems a little tired.

"Mr. Doe? I'm Henry Cox, Countrywide Mutual." His handshake is firm, if a bit moist. When you ask him in, he stands in your foyer and gives a knowing little shake of his head.

"Looks like a wonderful place you've got here," says Henry. That's an invitation for you to talk, to tell him about the house, about the smaller place you moved from, and all the rest—including, if you're a frank and open individual, the size of the monthly mortgage payments.

You take Mr. Cox's coat, for which he thanks you, and offer to lead him into the living room, where there's a comfortable sofa. He may follow you, but he may equally well surprise you by saying no.

"Mr. Doe, have you got a place where we could sit and relax at a table together?" Somewhat wonderingly, you accompany him into the kitchen, where he ensconces you at your breakfast table, taking a neighboring chair himself.

Henry Cox is a real professional. Like all good in-the-house salesmen, he knows that the kitchen is the heart of the home. ("More sales are made at the kitchen table than anywhere else!" his training manual advises.) Once Henry has you in your own kitchen, he's much more your friend than your guest—and you've taken the first big step closer to becoming his customer.

Now that you're sitting down comfortably together, you might think that Henry will steer the conversation toward life insurance. But Henry's too old a hand for that. Instead, he comments on how clean and neat the kitchen looks (if it's messy, he'll comment on your family's busy life and encourage you to tell him what a good cook your wife is). Or else Henry will make a remark or two about his new car, his children, or seemingly anything under the sun.

Far from being unpremeditated, Henry's conversation is carefully directed at making you feel that you both share some common *personal* ground.

This procedure is known as the Approach, and it's considered by shrewd salesmen to be an absolutely crucial step. In fact, the Approach requires the most delicate judgment and timing of any stage of the interview. Henry's introduction of himself will take just long enough to satisfy Henry that you're a normal, sound individual (and not, for example, somebody with a grudge against life insurance men or somebody obviously too ancient or too decrepit to insure). The introduction will also, Henry hopes, ease your anxiety about being face to face with a stranger who wants you to buy something. Finally, a properly timed introduction will reinforce your conviction that Henry belongs to the same "club" you do, that he's your sort of guy.

Having decided that these preliminaries have gone on exactly long enough, Henry leans forward in his chair and utters some such statement as:

"Mr. Doe, I'd like to draw you a little sketch that may

make a point or two about life insurance." A pad of paper and a pen make their appearance on the kitchen table—a pen, not a pencil. Henry's likely to need that pen later on, when papers may have to be signed.

To the life insurance sales expert, one picture is indeed worth a thousand words—and perhaps as many dollars. As your eye begins to follow the lines, circles, and squiggles of Henry's pen, you also begin to attend to his deliberately low-pitched voice. His first phrases have an innocuous ring. He may start with any of dozens of ideas; for example:

"Most men, in this day of high expenses and higher taxes, find it difficult to accumulate money . . ." or,

"Mr. Doe, suppose this slanting line represents a man's increasing responsibilities . . ." or,

"You know, Mr. Doe, a friend of mine said just the other day, 'Henry, how on earth do most people find a way to save . . .' "

And so ad infinitum, but not ad lib. Henry has begun to talk, not about you and your questions or problems, but about "most people." He's also begun to sell you life insurance, though at this point you're meant to be only dimly aware of the fact. What Henry wants is to pose a so-called "general problem" and *have you agree* that for most men the problem is a real one. So he finishes off his sketch with a flick of the pen and a perfectly timed question.

"As you can see then, most men can't solve this problem" —Henry slashes a line across his sketch—"if their time is cut short, can they, Mr. Doe?"

And you agree; most men can't solve their problem. "But what's this got to do with me?"

"I'm coming to that, Mr. Doe. Now, I would assume that like most men you already own some life insurance. Is that correct?"

We've seen that Henry is a good salesman, and at this

point he's proved it once again by shifting smoothly from what the industry calls "the general problem" to "the specific problem"—namely, you and your life insurance. At last, you think, he's come around to the reason I asked him to call on me, my present insurance. And you proceed to tell Henry whatever you know about the life insurance you now own. Henry listens attentively, his pen busily making notes as he watches your face.

"Hmmm. That's a total of thirty-five thousand dollars. Tell me, Mr. Doe, I assume you own this fine home rather than rent it?"

And Henry has diplomatically started to question *you* about your property and finances. He may ask how much you pay on your mortgage (in case you haven't told him), whether you or your wife expects to inherit any money, and similar questions—all in a casual, conversational manner. There's one question Henry will never ask, how much you make a month. He knows the delicate difference between routine questions about your status and prying into your personal financial condition, and Henry's much too seasoned a salesman to risk getting your back up. Besides, Henry doesn't have to ask. He's had a look at your home, he's probably familiar with your neighborhood, with the company you work for, and with the kind of job you hold. The chances are that Henry can gauge your salary accurately— within a few dollars a month anyway.

You go along with all of this without being quite sure where it's leading. You tell Henry your date of birth (that's basic information to a life insurance man), how old your wife and children are, and whatever else he asks you. But finally you grow a little impatient and ask Henry a direct question about your own life insurance; for example, how much money you've accumulated under one policy or whether your group life insurance at the office pays any dividends.

"We're coming to that point in just a couple of minutes!" Henry assures you earnestly. "But before we do, Mr. Doe, could I just ask you one question?" He pauses to make sure you're paying attention. "Do you know, Mr. Doe, that if you were taken out of the picture tonight, your family would have less than a third of your present income to live on while your children were growing up? And that Mary, as your widow, would have *nothing* once Barbara [your youngest] reached the age of eighteen?"

There are as many ways of taking the gloves off in a life insurance sales interview as there are insurance salesmen. Henry's method is not that of the shocked discoverer of your sad state of affairs ("I can't believe that a man like you would let that happen"). Nor does Henry indulge in finger-shaking admonition ("Take my word for it, Mr. Doe, your family's in trouble"). He belongs to a different, quieter sales breed. Henry presents his findings with the air of an auditor putting his finger on an awkward and potentially trouble-some shortage in one of your accounts. Because you're a businessman, and therefore presumably sensitive about money, Henry knows that this stratagem is exactly the right way to disturb you about your insurance situation.

And you are disturbed. What you thought would be an impersonal discussion of a few facts and figures has turned into a real problem session. Right away you want to know how Henry has arrived at his unhappy conclusions about your present insurance. Henry doesn't even have to consult the tables in that little black book which has also materi-alized on the kitchen table.

"Well, Mr. Doe, if you passed away tonight, your Social Security benefits would pay Mary a monthly income of two hundred and fifty-four dollars until your eldest reached age eighteen. Then that income would drop off to one-ninety a month until the youngest child reached the same age. After that, nothing until Mary reached sixty-two. Your present life insurance could be set up to add to that income. You've got about thirty-five thousand dollars of insurance. That's about two-fifty a month for the next fifteen years if you let the companies pay out the money as income. So taking everything into consideration, Mary and the kids would have a little less than five hundred a month to live on—and that wouldn't last forever."

That's the longest speech Henry's made so far, and according to the sales pattern he's following, it's the pivotal speech of the evening. Henry has introduced himself, secured your agreement on some "general problem" that most men share, and aroused you to the existence of a "specific problem" belonging to you and you alone. Having stirred you up, Henry's perfectly willing to answer one or two questions about life insurance; it keeps the pot boiling. So Henry fills you in on a few details of your National Service Life Insurance and explains the temporary nature of your group coverage. But Henry knows he's got you agitated, and after a few minutes of letting the pressure build up, he says:

"Mr. Doe, if there were a plan which would let you increase the amount of income you'd be leaving to your family in case you die, and if this plan would also solve some of your other future financial needs—such as money to give your children the kind of education they deserve—wouldn't such a plan be an ideal solution for your problem?"

Now Henry has started to sell out in the open. Sure it would solve my problem, you tell him. But what with the house, and the kid's orthodonture to pay for, and perhaps a new car, you just can't afford even to consider any more life

12·

insurance right now. Maybe in six months, when that bonus comes through—

You don't know it, but you've already sold yourself. You've admitted the *need* for more insurance, and a salesman as alert as Henry knows that this is half the battle. He's persuaded you to accept the idea that more life insurance (and not some other alternative) is the answer, and he's ready now for the next step in his campaign: to answer your objections, and in the language of salesmanship, "motivate" you to take action right away.

"Mr. Doe, I'd be astonished if you were in any position right now to lay out a substantial amount of money to solve this problem. Most men"—notice Henry's adroit shift of pressure away from you and your troubles—"are unable to write a blank check. But tell me something. Could you save a hundred dollars a month to put into insurance?"

No, you tell him, of course not.

"Could you set aside a dollar a month?"

Yes, you guess you could pretty easily.

"Mr. Doe, there's an amount somewhere between a dollar a month and a hundred dollars a month that you could put aside to solve your problem, isn't there?"

The process of persuading you to name a definite amount is known in selling as Getting the Commitment. Henry figures you can afford to spend four or five dollars a week for more insurance. So he sets his little trap, and you spring it by permitting yourself to think for the first time in terms of hard cash. Unless Henry can coax this commitment out of you—this specific amount of money that you might ("I didn't say that you *would* . . .") part with—he knows he's in for trouble because you might evade him later on.

But you make things easy for Henry, partly because you feel that maybe you do need more life insurance, and partly because, dammit, you can't bring yourself to admit to Henry that a few paltry dollars a week would be any problem to find.

"Now let me give you some idea of what that five dollars a week would do for your family." Henry flips open his little black book (unless he's a virtuoso who can carry rough figures in his head). After some moments of scrawling numbers on his pad, Henry looks up at you and proclaims triumphantly:

"Mr. Doe, five dollars a week will do quite a job. It will provide enough life insurance to send your youngsters to college—$10,000. In addition, it will increase that income you're leaving from five hundred to six hundred dollars a month until the children are eighteen, and then give your wife housekeeping money of a hundred and fifty dollars a month until her Social Security begins. And not only that, Mr. Doe. When you get to the normal retirement age of sixty-five, the company will give you nine thousand dollars in cash or an income of fifty dollars a month for the rest of your life. Doesn't that seem like a pretty good proposition to you?"

Henry pauses. If he's handled himself properly, your answer has to be "Yes," and his next question will be, "Mr. Doe, when's the last time you visited a doctor?" In other words, Henry will have begun to fill out his company's life insurance application form.

However, human nature being perverse, Henry knows you may answer "Yes, but—" Depending on the reason for your reluctance, Henry will produce one or another of his favorite motivating devices—a story or an anecdote or perhaps an actual physical prop. He may show you a chart demonstrating what a good thing it is for children to go to college. If he thinks you're greedy, Henry may stress that a goodly portion of the money you put into this plan will be returned to you when you're ready to retire. All such motivating material is designed to assuage the fears which supposedly lurk behind your surface objections, to reassure you and pave the way for a smooth "close" of the sale.

Because you're reasonably sophisticated and decisive, Henry doesn't need to go to extremes. He can save his supply of tear-jerking stories for another kind of customer. With you, Henry can proceed smoothly to the final steps. You help him fill in the application form ("I'll just complete this in my office"); you sign your name; you even write out a small check ("Twenty-six dollars and fifty cents puts this plan in force the minute our doctor approves you"). In case you do balk somewhere along the line, Henry may tell you a joke or ask you another question. If you display a great deal of last-minute recalcitrance, he may take you back step by step, with inexorable logic, over all the points you agreed to previously; then he'll simply hand you his pen, sit back, and wait. The chances are that you'll docilely sign the form, write the check, and agree to be examined by the company doctor.

After promising to be in touch ("As soon as I have approval from the home office, I'll let you know"), Henry gathers up all of his papers (thus leaving nothing behind which a competitor might attack) and stuffs them in his briefcase. He takes with him all your other life insurance policies, promising to "prepare for your files" an outline and color chart of their benefits.

"Get the order and run" is the standard routine in selling, for fear the customer might change his mind; so Henry doesn't linger. He shakes your hand, says good night, and departs. Your evidence that he's been there is a receipt for your check and a business card. But he'll be back to deliver your policy and collect the balance of money due. You're his newest "client"—until the next successful sales interview.

Henry has committed no crime, perpetrated no fraud. Nor have you been duped or become the victim of a swindle. On the contrary, you and Henry have jointly begun to work out an arrangement that could be of great benefit to your family in case, in Henry's delicate phrase, you were "taken out of the picture." So when you think back over the evening, perhaps you feel only a warm glow of satisfaction at having faced and solved a serious problem. But even as you congratulate yourself on your foresight, prudence, and financial maturity, it's also possible that you feel a twinge of uneasiness. Five dollars a week doesn't *seem* like much money, but it does add up. A minute's work with a pencil will show you that in fact it adds up to thousands of dollars over the years. If you carry this insurance for the thirty years until your retirement, you'll have socked away no less than $7,800 of after-tax money—by most standards, a sizable chunk of cash.

At this point it may strike you that you'd like to know a lot more than you've been told about what you're getting for that money. If Henry had sold you an encyclopedia, a dishwasher, or an automobile, the tangible product itself would gleam brand-new in your home or garage to reassure you that your transaction was indeed for value received. But a life insurance policy has no such material solidity to soothe your doubts. Therefore, you might well wonder, What exactly have I bought?

And you may also wonder about the smooth way Henry eased you into the sale. Was it really necessary for him to be so persuasive and tell so little? As he slides behind the wheel of his car, Henry, you may be absolutely certain, feels no such unease. But is his the pleasurable pride of having helped a fellow man resolve his difficulties—or a somewhat different pleasure at having knocked off another pigeon ("That's my quota for this week") and made a couple of hundred dollars into the bargain?

As you ponder the evening's result you may put aside your questions as naïve or not really important. After all, Henry seems like a decent, honest man, and Countrywide Mutual is a big, reputable insurance company. Surely it's absurd to worry. But all the same, it is hard to avoid being curious, especially because Henry now occupies, along with your lawyer and your banker, a position of trust in your scheme of things. So those nagging questions still remain. What *is* life insurance all about? And what sort of man is Henry Cox? Does he really have your interests at heart?

"People are stupid, you hear?
So don't explain, just con them a little."
—the Manager

2 . *What's Really in That Policy?*

WITH SURPRISING EXACTNESS, the little drama of the life insurance sale mirrors the much broader drama of the way the
industry operates in public and in private. The seemingly
simple doubts raised in your mind by your encounter with
Henry lead directly to the complex, serious problems that
surround the entire institution of life insurance. For this
immense industry rests on that individual sale—on Henry
versus you repeated tens of millions of times every year. Before we start to scrutinize the industry's inner workings, we
have good reason to take a closer look at this small-scale
situation, briefly in terms of the buyer and seller and at
greater length in terms of what is actually bought and sold.

When you stop to think about it, the process by which you
bought life insurance didn't really involve consideration of
the product at all. Henry has been trained to *avoid* any specific discussion of the nature of life insurance, and he sincerely believes that the facts and figures—the plain truth—
will only get in the way and complicate his job.

Henry's viewpoint, which is that of almost every salesman,

19 ·

actually grows out of two rather peculiar assumptions: first, that as far as the basic facts about insurance are concerned, you already know as much as you need to know; and second, that you aren't interested in what life insurance *is*, but only what it *does* for you and your family. In short, life insurance is so simple that a man is born understanding the matter. At the same time, life insurance is so complicated that trying to explain it only interferes with getting people to buy it.

Because life insurance men cling to this curious mystique, almost everything they say to the public is confusing and even self-contradictory. Worse yet, the way Henry and his fellow salesmen say things about life insurance is designed to hide, rather than to clarify, the real issues. Later we'll see why this is the case. But right now let's glance at a few examples.

Typically every life insurance salesman refers to a given insurance arrangement as a "plan." The customer who owns more than one insurance plan is the possessor of a life insurance "program." Under this plan or program, a man "carries" a given amount of "protection." But his plan may also offer "living values" as well as "provide security" for his family "in case something happens."

Such vague terminology is based entirely on the idea that you only want to know what insurance *does*. This, of course, is the legendary American language of sales promotion, of "Sell the Sizzle, Not the Steak." In life insurance, sales-promotion language reaches the floweriest heights of rhetoric and bristles with pompous, pseudo-impressive phraseology. Insurance men do exactly what the realtor does when he calls a mortgage a "lifetime equity system," a wonderfully juicy phrase for a long-term debt.

These rotundities of speech certainly don't add much to

your understanding of life insurance. But on the other hand, life insurance men are equally prone to converse with their customers about "premiums," "dividend additions," "beneficiaries," "optional modes of settlement," and so on into the thicket of technical verbiage. Whenever a salesman delivers the policy he's sold—and tries to collect for it—such technicalities seem to pour from his lips, doubtless because this is his way of making his product sound important to the customer. But there is another reason these terms are used freely. The salesman believes that you already know enough about life insurance to understand exactly what he's talking about. And never mind that this technical language of insurance is if anything more baffling than the glossy jargon of sales promotion.

Of course, the real masterpieces of non-communication between the industry and the customer are those letters, brochures, and other sales literature which draw heavily on both vocabularies.

To look at this problem from your own point of view, you can have heard a great deal of talk and read your way through page after page of so-called explanation—and yet not understand the most basic and essential features of life insurance. This isn't your fault, but the industry's; and such partial enlightenment is almost worse than complete ignorance. Almost everybody knows the obvious: a life insurance policy pays off when the insured person dies. (But how much does it pay? How are those payments arranged? Who gets the money?) Some people also realize that certain life insurance policies provide for the insured individual to collect money during his own lifetime in the form of cash equities. It's also fairly well grasped that as age increases the rates for insurance go up and that insurance can sometimes be borrowed against (though people still ask why the life insurance company charges interest "to lend a man his own money"). Finally, most people are aware that if they don't pay on time, their policies will "lapse" and cease to be effective.

These particulars sum up almost everything most people actually know about life insurance. Possession of this pocketful of assorted facts usually doesn't hurt anybody. But as many an insurance owner has discovered to his dismay, when the need to figure out life insurance becomes pressing, as it inevitably does, that slender inventory of facts isn't very helpful.

Some measure of relief is available from another and very different kind of language, that of the law. To the layman, legal language seems formidable; but nevertheless, it can present certain unvarnished and interesting facts about life insurance. Besides, it's extremely important to remember that a life insurance policy is, among other things, a legal agreement—a written, enforceable contract between a policy owner and an insurance company.

As a matter of fact, the word "policy" is derived from the Italian word *polizza*, which originally meant "promise" or "undertaking." The Venetians used that term first to signify any legal document and later to designate the elaborately inscribed parchments which proved to insurance-minded Venice that coverage was in force. The other modern descendant of the word *polizza* is popular in the underworld, which refers to the numbers racket as "the policy game," to numbers tickets as "policy slips," and so on. The parallel terminology is probably more than a coincidence, because insurance shares with organized gambling a common origin in the mathematics of probability.

Thus, one term lawyers use to describe the contractual nature of life insurance is "aleatory." An insurance policy is an aleatory (or wagering) contract, like a bet on a horse race, because in either case there exists the chance of a large return from a small investment. All such betting propositions, life insurance included, are obviously vulnerable to fraud. So much of the verbiage contained in that thick sheaf of pages which almost nobody reads—the insurance policy itself—is designed to protect each party against the consequences of deliberate fraud by the other.

By glancing at other legal concepts peculiar to life insurance contracts, we can see that contract law both safeguards and clarifies the agreement. Besides being "aleatory," an insurance contract is "unilateral" (because under its terms, only the insurance company makes a truly enforceable promise); "conditional" (because the company has to pay off only if certain conditions are met, death being one of the conditions); a contract of "adhesion" (because neither the company nor the insured party has the right to haggle over terms); and a "stated sum" contract (because a fixed amount of money is involved).

To anyone who worries about the fine print in a legal document, such concepts may sound ominous. But just because the life insurance contract is as precise and airtight as lawyers can make it doesn't necessarily mean that the policy is a legal trap. It's worth pointing out here that every phrase in the insurance contract has undergone and will always be subject to practical tests for fairness in the courts. To the discomfiture of the industry, American courts lean toward liberal interpretations of life insurance policies in favor of the insurance owner. The steady pressure of law has helped to make these contracts both safe and equitable for the customer, so that whatever is wrong with life insurance, it's not the policy itself. The surprisingly simple sentence that makes the policy contract valid and effective rings with a certain dignity.

The Company WILL PAY the Face Amount to the Beneficiary upon receipt of due proof of the Insured's Death, subject to the provisions on the following pages of this Policy.

You may have trouble finding this "insuring clause" amid all the scrollwork and engraving on the front of the policy, but it's there, absolutely unequivocal.

Even this brief venture into the legal background of the life insurance policy should clear the air of sales jargon and technical pedantry. Now it should be easier to deal directly with the principles embodied in every policy and also come to grips with the theories behind insurance itself.

Life insurance is essentially a simple creation. Its "raw materials" consist of information which can easily be printed on a single sheet of paper. All that's needed to construct any form of life insurance is (1) a table that shows the number of people living and dying from age zero to age one hundred out of a given sampling of the population, and (2) another table, this one a set of interest figures similar to what bankers use. The interest table merely indicates how much a dollar will be worth in a given number of years at a given rate of interest. With these two statistical aggregations, as commonplace today as the multiplication table, you can fabricate any life insurance scheme and compute its cost.

Similarly, there *seem* to be as many kinds of life insurance as there are pebbles on the beach. But this apparently endless variety can be sorted into two basic types. Insurance companies are convinced that the public has no taste for simplicity, so as a matter of marketing philosophy, they keep combining and recombining these basic forms. But to an insurance man's eye, the "exciting new plans" have a dreadful sameness. Real innovation is rare almost to the point of non-existence.

An entire chapter could be devoted to the picturesque

names which life insurance marketers give their policies. The rhetoric of insurance marketing currently favors such status-enhancing policy titles as "The Executive Special," "The Professional Equity," and "The Preferred Accumulator." This nomenclature is obviously supposed to confer prestige on both policy and policy owner, but since insurance sales-men almost never mention policy titles to their customers, the effectiveness of impressive-sounding titles is dubious.

And whatever the package or its label, life insurance comes in only two forms.

The first kind of life insurance works like this. If the in-sured dies within a given period of time, the company pays the agreed sum of money to the insured's designee. The period of time can be any length at all: a year, five years, ten years (or longer)—or twenty minutes if the company will go along. But once the insured lives beyond the specified period, he's no longer insured. It's as if he bet the cost of the policy against the much larger amount he's insured for that he'd die within a stated period—and lost his bet because he lived. So the company keeps his money, and both parties are quits.

This method of insuring is known as "term insurance" because of the limited length of time, called the "term," over which it's effective. Term insurance is the oldest and simplest form of life insurance. Such straightforward protection against death would have remained the only form available had it not been for one problem: the cost of term insurance increases greatly as men grow older.

A man might well discover as his insurance nears an end that his need for insurance will continue. In that case, he'll have to insure himself all over again for a new term.

But in starting over again, there's one difference: he's older. The first statistical table mentioned earlier—the "mortality table," to call it by its trade name—naturally demonstrates an ever increasing number of deaths as its sample population climbs the year-by-year steps from age zero to one hundred (the age at which, statistically speaking, everybody's dead). So for a man insuring his life over again at a later age, the same amount of insurance will cost more money, since the risk of death is greater.

Furthermore, mortality accelerates rapidly as a given age group gets older. So the cost of term insurance not only rises, but rises by bigger and bigger differentials. At the high end of the age scale, a man approaches the literally fatal point where he'd have to pay as much money to the insurance company as the company would pay his survivors when he died. If a man needs life insurance not for a few years but for an indefinite, unpredictable length of time, he has to face the distasteful fact that the cost of his insurance will go up and up forever.

For example, at twenty-five $100,000 worth of life insurance for a term of five years costs a mere $400 a year. At thirty the same amount costs only $429. By thirty-five the annual outlay has increased to $500. Skipping a few intermediate stages brings us to age fifty, when the same policy costs a somewhat startling $1,388 a year. At fifty-five the price is $2,086; and from sixty (when many companies refuse to sell such insurance at any price) to sixty-five the annual cost is $3,186. Beyond sixty-five this kind of life insurance is fairly rare and—in terms of its starting point at least—very expensive.

Human nature lends an ironic twist to the problem of high insurance costs. Faced with the inevitable rise in the outlay for term insurance, healthy men are apt to give up the idea of insuring themselves at the older ages. But people whose health gives them reason to worry will hang on to their life insurance no matter what the cost. So the poorer risks remain insured.

Remember that mortality tables, on which insurance rates are based, have been computed from a cross section of the population. More deaths will occur among insurance customers than these standard tables allow for; insured but ailing lives will be beating the company's odds by dying too soon and too often. This disquieting phenomenon, known as "anti-selection," drives the price of term insurance even higher at the older ages—and as a result, of course, even fewer healthy people will decide that the insurance is worth the price. In practice, such a spiraling effect makes it tough to make a profit on term insurance without elaborate, expensive, and sales-dampening precautions against getting caught in the spiral.

It goes without saying that for the customer, this inescapable rise in the cost of life insurance is almost as grim to contemplate as death itself. It seems outrageous to be confronted with such an expense at the end, as if it weren't enough to have to die. It's one thing to convince a man that insuring his life is a good idea, but another matter entirely to talk him into accepting lifelong inflation in the price of his protection. Historically there had to be a solution to this dilemma or there couldn't have been a life insurance industry at all.

As early as the eighteenth century, some idea of the proper solution had occurred to the early advocates of life insurance. But it took nearly a century and a half for the rough-hewn beginnings to be shaped into a workable form—the second basic type of life insurance. To understand this second kind of life insurance isn't as difficult as most people think, as long as the following pattern of facts is kept in mind.

(1) People die.

(2) It's impossible to predict the length of an individual life.

(3) However, given the numbers of people living and dying at all ages (in other words, a mortality table), it is possible statistically to predict the *average* life expectancy at any age.

(4) Once such an average life expectancy is figured, it's not hard to compute the cost of term insurance, starting at a given age, for each successive year until the *whole length* of life is completely insured, that length being based on the average.

(5) Once each year's term-insurance cost is calculated, arriving at the *total cost* of any amount of life insurance is a matter of adding up the individual costs, which will, of course, be lower near the starting age and higher later on.

(6) By essentially the same process bankers use in figuring interest on a loan (here's where that second table of interest rates comes in), it's then possible to figure out how much money is needed *today* to cover the inevitable death claim later on, assuming that the money earns a given rate of interest during the intervening years.

Having acquired the necessary statistical techniques, life insurance pioneers were able to develop this beautifully simple way of extending the length of insurance from a fixed term to the whole of life; and thus, they created the second form of insurance from the first.

This discovery meant that the basic problem of spiraling insurance costs could be immensely simplified. In fact, this problem turned out to be nothing more than the question of how to pay for a lifetime's worth of insurance in one fixed sum. Once they had solved this easier problem, these technicians found it just as easy to produce formulas for *spreading* the fixed cost *evenly* over any period of time desired. This in turn brought the price of insurance within everybody's

reach because a man could arrange payments for his life insurance that would never increase as he grew older.

So for a long time it's been possible—and sometimes
clever—for an individual to pay the entire present and future
cost of his life insurance in a single big installment. The
total cost (or "single premium") for $100,000 of permanent
(or "whole of life") insurance at twenty-five is $38,632, ac-
cording to one company's figures. There's a certain amount
of padding included to take care of the company's "non-
mortality" expenses. But roughly speaking, the figure represents the company's estimate of how much money it needs
now to pay the eventual death claim of $100,000. The in-
surance company assumes that the insured will live long
enough for the company to earn $61,368 of interest on the
money paid in today. That's the kind of assumption you
make only if you're an insurance company. (The company's
chances do look a little better, however, when you realize
that the current mortality table gives a man aged twenty-five
another 45.82 years to live.)

In certain special situations, mostly involving wealthy men
with big tax problems, such single-shot arrangements are
useful. But most people prefer to take a little longer—or a
lot longer—to pay. By now, it will be obvious to a great many
readers, we're back on familiar ground. For the individual
who decides to spread the cost of his permanent insurance
over his entire lifetime is buying the so-called "ordinary life
insurance" policy, which is the staple of the industry.*

Between the two extremes of permanent insurance—"pay
it all at once" and "pay until you die"—you can handle the

---

* For the record, if that $100,000 term-insurance policy (see page 26)
had been bought instead for the whole of life, it would have cost about
$1,700 a year at age twenty-five, with level installments all the way down
the line.

installments as flexibly as a given company will permit. Some insurance buyers don't want to "pay until I die." It's easy to set up a schedule of payments over a shorter fixed period— twenty years being a favorite—so that the whole cost of insurance can be budgeted into a peak earning span. (The companies love these "limited payment" plans because they bring in the full payment years in advance of death; but limited-payment policies are getting harder to sell.)

So the whole-of-life concept, which first became feasible about a hundred and fifty years ago, made life insurance into a prototype of the easy-payment installment plan. In fact, this century-and-a-half-old experiment in buying on time has taught a host of industries with expensive goods for sale how to handle such financing.

A reasonably sharp-eyed reader (and most of those with any insurance-buying experience) will have noticed an interesting—and ultimately crucial—fact. The installment-payment method of buying permanent insurance costs more initially than term insurance does. Pay-until-you-die coverage, at the rate of $1,700 per $100,000 of insurance, is more than four times as expensive at age twenty-five as five-year term insurance. Does this mean that permanent insurance is a bad buy?

Not really.

A moment's reflection shows that as an old man, our twenty-five-year-old might have to pay $4,000 or more a year for the latest—perhaps the last—in his series of five-year term contracts. But had he bought permanent insurance instead, he would have to lay out only $1,700 a year no matter how long he lived. The initial overpayment is necessary so that years later, when the cost of term insurance becomes so alarmingly high, the customer can *underpay*.

Later we'll find out whether or not this initial "overcharge"—and for that matter, all life insurance pricing—is reasonable. Right now the key question is, What happens to the extra money the customer pays to the insurance company during those early years?

Obviously the company must do something with this money until it is needed to pay the inevitable death claim. The important thing to remember is that for the company as for the individual, money begets money in the form of interest. Most individuals think of interest as the modest sum earned yearly on a savings account or the price paid for a loan. But after emergencies (or buying sprees) have reduced the savings account to a shadow of its former self, the interest earnings seem barely enough to buy a cup of coffee. Or when, thank God, the loan is finally paid off, those interest charges are hardly worth remembering. To most people, interest is a fact of which to be fleetingly aware, but one which makes very little long-term difference.

However, when that lone twenty-five-year-old who at first overpaid to buy the presumably more sensible permanent insurance is multiplied ten millionfold, and when still more millions of his younger and older cousins are added in, the life insurance industry's affection for its interest tables becomes understandable. It's simply that the extra money paid into life insurance companies by their customers earns interest not for a couple of years but for decades.

A twenty-five-year-old will live another 45.82 years; a thirty-five-year-old can be expected to live 36.69 more years; even a seventy-five-year-old will probably live another 7.81 years. Such beautiful longevity statistics mean that life insurance companies will always be repositories for huge sums that won't be reclaimed for a long, long time. At least, such will be the case as long as the thousands of life insurance owners dying each year (and leaving survivors who collect) are replaced by thousands more young, healthy buyers who can be counted on to pay and pay for years.

That's why the industry employs 500,000 salesmen.

It goes without saying that life insurance companies do not own the billions of dollars entrusted to them as "reserves" against their future costs of death. Such reserves are scrupulously segregated from the company's own assets because the reserves are in fact debts owed by the insurance company to its customers—debts collectable at death.

But the industry can afford to be scrupulous about money because the *use* of these reserves, the obligation to invest such a mountain of money for so long a time, is a golden opportunity for the industry's component companies.

To remain solvent, an insurance company needs to earn, in good years and bad, only a nice safe 2.5 or 3 per cent. But what if the company's management earns the relatively modest return of, say, 4 per cent on its total assets? In 1965 even savings banks paid a higher rate than that.

A dollar invested at 2.5 per cent is worth only $1.05 after two years. But that same dollar invested at 2.5 per cent for twenty-five years—not a long time for a life insurance company—is worth $1.85. Its value has practically doubled. That's a substantial benefit for the dollar's real owner, the life insurance buyer. But at 4 per cent over twenty-five years a dollar is worth $2.67. In other words, each dollar invested at 4 per cent interest today is worth $1.85 to the insurance customer in twenty-five years—and another $.85 to the company—which is a lot of extra vigorish, as other and less legitimate odds-players like to put it. Obviously, a quarter, an eighth, or even a sixteenth of a percentage point is well worth struggling for if you're a life insurance company.

It's equally obvious that time and compound interest confer enormous earning power on such companies. Small wonder the state laws that govern life insurance in this country include strict limitations on the industry's freedom to invest the public's dollars. But short of driving the insurance companies out of business and literally crippling the nation's economy, there's no way state legislatures can prevent the eternal cornerstones of economic life—time and interest—from making these companies richer and richer.

So incredible were the opportunities for enrichment in the industry's earlier and palmier days, that long ago the biggest life insurance companies had to save themselves from a day of public reckoning. This they did by "mutualizing," which, roughly speaking, turns an insurance company from a profit-making private corporation into a kind of vast profit-sharing association. Since the turn of the century, company after company has accepted mutualization more or less voluntarily. (Some companies were even mutualized from the start by their founders.)

In a mutual company the policyholders are deemed to own the company. In theory, they, and not stockholders, get the benefit of the company's investment acumen—in the form of "dividends," which have the effect of reducing insurance costs over the years. Today most of the big life insurance companies are mutual companies, ostensibly dividing their profits among the millions of people who own insurance with the given company.

But even in a mutual company, management decides what dividends, if any, shall be paid out. And precisely because the "ownership" of a mutual company is diffused among so very many thousands of individual insurance buyers, the control of the company is more tightly vested in management than is the case even in the most narrowly run stock corporation. Indeed, mutual policyholders have never—not even in the beginning, when companies were small—been able to vote themselves bigger dividends, lower rates, or better management. And you can be certain that present-day management will preserve that enviable autocracy at no matter what price to the public.

It's hardly necessary to add one point. From time to time, sensationalists have accused the entire American life insurance industry of defrauding the public. As we shall see, there is certainly a conspiratorial flavor in the way insurance-company management acts. But that conspiracy is not designed to cheat us out of our money. Any sane man who has considered the nature of life insurance will realize that from the viewpoint of industry management, there's no *reason* to cheat. It's much easier to adhere scrupulously to the letter of the financial contract and much more lucrative to be honest.

And so, over the past hundred and fifty years, the permanent, whole-of-life, installment-paid concept of insurance has produced (1) a convenient way for the individual to insure himself for the rest of his days; (2) the packaging of life insurance as a palatable, plausible scheme that could be marketed to millions and millions of consumers; and (3) a set of tremendous private companies competing with one another for the biggest prize our free enterprise system has to offer, perpetual control of hundreds of billions of dollars of the public's money.

Let's glance back briefly to the turn of the century, to see what this industry, then already fifty years old, had managed to accomplish. In 1900 the total assets of the nation's life insurance companies amounted to some $2,000,000,000. In that year 126 companies sold Americans about $1,500,-000,000 worth of new life insurance. And of these companies, only a few were large and aggressive.

Today the numbers are different. There are now nearly

1,700 companies in the life insurance business, selling about $95,000,000,000 worth of insurance each year. They range from small outfits with fewer than a thousand customers to behemoths like the Metropolitan, which estimates that it insures 45,000,000 people. A given company may do business in an area no wider than its local community or it may blanket the entire continent and branch out overseas. Each of the fifty states now boasts at least two life insurance companies.

Patterns of operation vary, from crude solicitation out of one small, dingy office to marketing empires far too vast for any centralized control. There are companies that sell exclusively to Negroes, to Chinese-Americans, to Puerto Ricans, to military officers, to college graduates, to non-smokers and teetotalers, and to many other special groups. There are so-called fraternal orders whose primary purpose is to insure the lives of their members. Some companies sell solely to such captive customers as installment-credit buyers, mutual-fund purchasers, or mortgage-holders.

But despite this genuine diversity, the bulk of the nation's life insurance is controlled by about 200 companies, the industry's oldest, largest, and financially strongest. Of these, 156 are giant mutual enterprises, and the remainder are owned by stockholders. The "top 200" sell approximately 90 per cent of all the insurance marketed in this country. These are the companies whose agents we expect to call on us, whose advertising appears on television and in the national magazines. These are the companies that set the pace for the entire industry. And for better or worse, these are the companies whose methods and standards of doing business the public must accept in order to have life insurance.

The next few chapters will explore the methods, practices, and philosophies of these big companies, which together exercise that curious combination of hotly competitive and yet oligarchic trade we know to be typical of American industry. Let's start with the distribution of life insurance—with how this industry actually sells us our insurance.

"We like them better when they're running scared."

—*the Recruiter*

3 . *"Hell, We'll Hire Any Warm Body"*

IN ORDER TO GET YOU—and 20,000,000 other people a year —to buy life insurance, every major insurance company is deeply committed to one technique only: the use of salesmen. Clearly, no industry committed to mass marketing on so vast a scale can possibly afford to depend on the efforts of a few supersalesmen. There simply aren't enough such men to go around. As far back as the turn of the century the market for life insurance had proved far too vast to be exploited only by the natural-born sales artists. So even before 1900 this industry had spawned a complex organization known as the American Agency System, which could make use of the average man's abilities and capacities as a salesman. In theory—and there's nothing wrong with the theory —that's what any growing business has to do in order to keep on growing.

But life insurance isn't just any business.

In the first place, life insurance is too complicated for the average man to learn to sell. Second, and even more important, the average man cannot stand the physical and emotional strains of selling insurance. For most men, the frustration and rejection inherent in the job prove too severe to endure.

So an industry intent only on pushing ahead saw, and still sees, only one choice: to get the maximum possible mileage out of *unsuccessful* salesmen. The men who staff and operate the Agency System are taught, and later teach their successors, that it's necessary to enlist and exploit men whom they suspect and often know in advance will be total failures at selling life insurance. For the record, total failure means just that: the inability to earn a subsistence-level income which would pay the rent and put food on the table.

But there's more to this matter than the scandal of how the life insurance industry, through the Agency System, acquires, trains, and controls hundreds upon hundreds of thousands of salesmen. Because of this system, *both you and your salesman* have only the most tenuous relationship with the company that provides the life insurance. Because of this system, your own agent may be a failure—but more to the point, your life insurance is only a shadowy promise of what it could and should be. And yet, without the American Agency System, life insurance as we know it couldn't exist at all.

In a big company the Agency System is entrenched in the sales division. The Sales Department is headed by a senior officer whose subordinates are themselves vice-presidents. Each regional vice-president is in turn superior to district superintendents who purportedly supervise—and at least keep in touch with—the "line" executives in the field. Branch offices (or agencies) are spread out over the local, regional, or national areas in which the given company operates. Such agencies cluster in big cities, where one company alone might establish dozens of small-sized agencies, each in theory covering a territory of a few city blocks. Today agencies have sprouted in the suburbs also, where so many customers are now located. But the important companies serve even the least populous parts of the country through a sizable agency network. In all, there are tens of thousands of life insurance agencies. According to the census data available, only gasoline stations, restaurants, laundries, and other small retail establishments outnumber them.

Each agency is run by a manager. In the early days of the industry, the manager was a completely independent businessman, or general agent. His franchise simply provided that he would sell—usually on an exclusive basis—a given quota of life insurance for the given company. His methods of operation and his finances were his own business, and the company paid him a flat commission for every dollar of insurance premium he collected. But today most companies make salary arrangements with agency managers, keeping these field executives at least nominally within the domain of the company's sales organization.

The manager is the key man in the Agency System, for he's the one who controls the destinies of the men who do the selling. The manager hires these men, signing as the company's representative the legal contract that authorizes the salesmen themselves to act as agents for the company. The manager supposedly determines how all his salesmen should operate and trains new salesmen to work effectively. And it's the manager who has the authority to cancel a salesman's contract and thereby sever the man's business relationship with the company. The agency manager exercises more authority over his charges than most non-insurance executives, no matter how high up, ever wield.

The reciprocal duties and obligations of the manager and the company are prescribed by company rules and spelled out in contracts. But the rulebook can't cover everything. Moreover, in psychological as well as physical distance, the manager's local realm is far, far away from the company's home office. Unless there's a crisis, the manager will have a free hand in running his operation. Both company and manager want it that way, and if things were different, the Agency System couldn't function. For the manager of a life insurance agency has only one basic job: to increase sales—this year, next year, and forever. The company doesn't really want to know what the manager does in order to keep on grinding out more and more new insurance—and the manager doesn't want the company to know. Therefore, between the agency manager and his superiors there's always the same unspoken (and certainly unwritten) agreement: keep on exceeding your assigned sales quotas, and you can write your own rules. Don't do anything blatantly fraudulent if you can help it; but above all, don't get caught.

One or more assistant managers is almost always at the manager's beck and call. Such assistants are managers in miniature, each one in charge of his own "unit," a group of up to ten salesmen. Assistant managers—who are all supposed to be longing for the day when they're given their own agencies—supervise the daily, and in some cases the hourly, routines of their men. In addition, as we'll soon discover, these junior executives have other highly significant duties.

One activity which all the agency's executives share is that of selling life insurance. Managers want to make themselves look good by adding their own sales to those of their salesmen. Also, selling is one way of earning extra money that meets with complete company approval. "Personal field work encourages the management team to keep its sales skills fresh," one management training manual says demurely. Because new salesmen "only respect managers who can do as well as teach," such personal selling supposedly makes it easier to train new men. So even if his management tasks do take up most of his time, a manager seldom hangs up his hat and quits selling altogether.

Finally, at the bottom of the ladder, we find—or we expect to find—the salesman himself. But unlike the agency manager and his assistants, the cashier, or even the girl who runs the switchboard, the insurance salesman is *not* an employee of the company he represents. Although you probably don't know it—and although your salesman himself may never have been told in so many words—the man who sells you your insurance is actually an "independent contractor," an entrepreneur running his own one-man business. Far more than even the lowliest typist or clerk, he is at the mercy of the manager and the company. He can be fired without the right of appeal, his business can be taken away, his career ended. His own rights are vague, and nowhere defined. In fact, his legal status is precisely that of a sharecropper or other contract laborer. And the treatment he gets from the company exactly reflects his status.

To substantiate this unsavory state of affairs and thus to understand the real nature of the salesman's lot, we must do our probing at the agency level—the level where a truly successful salesman is a rare bird indeed. Here's where the truth about the insurance business is really to be found, because the agency is designed to be a mill where through an endless process of enticement, trickery, and coercion, ordinary men are either converted into insurance salesmen or discarded. As we'll see, that process, starting from the beginning, is a mixture of comedy and anguish.

With the Agency System at its disposal, the company needs no special personnel department to select and recruit salesmen. That job is left entirely in the hands of the agency manager and his assistants, who have no choice but to be charming, persuasive, and ruthlessly dedicated exponents of insurance-selling as a career. The hunt for new salesmen will consume much of management's time and sweat. Holidays and weekends, when even the hardiest salesmen may temporarily rest from the wars, the manager must be interviewing prospective salesmen, either experienced men new to his company or absolutely raw recruits. On the surface, the manager's methods should seem like the legitimate routines of any employer with jobs to offer. None of his techniques can appear to be unscrupulous. But nevertheless, recruiting methods and the philosophy behind them will come as a jolt to the uninitiated.

For example, the smart manager will cultivate everyone in town who might steer prospective salesmen his way. Ministers, educators, and social leaders all make good "nominators" of potential recruits. Such "centers of influence" are cultivated mostly with blarney but sometimes with gifts or cash. For each situation the manager will work out a special approach.

He'll also build up his own private grapevine to keep abreast of any discontent among his competitors' salesmen. If he does any personal selling, he'll use his best salesmanship to extract the names of likely sales candidates from his customers—and at the same time proselytize the customers to become salesmen themselves. He'll use anything from back-scratching to subtle blackmail among his friends and *their* friends. A hungry manager on the prowl for new recruits makes his own salesmen seem genteel by comparison. One manager even teaches a night-school insurance course, "strictly because I can do eighty per cent of my recruiting right in class."

In training his assistants, the manager will sometimes instruct them to take charge of the agency's head-hunting for a given period. Assistant managers may be matched against one another to see who can bring in the most new men. Often each assistant is given a quota to fill on behalf of his own unit.

With the enthusiastic approval of the company, many

managers offer a bounty of $50 or $100 to an established salesman for each seriously interested candidate he turns up.

In a small town, where the local agency manager is likely to be prominent, more personal recruiting methods are generally the most effective. A clever and persuasive manager can get away with audacities which would make a run-of-the-mill recruiter a laughingstock. But he must also be careful about his recruiting so he won't have to face the accusing stares of local men who have failed after being talked into the life insurance business.

The real head-hunting and body-snatching in life insurance recruitment, and the most unprincipled hustling, all go on in the large cities, where the process of filling up the agency's roster of "rookie" salesmen is almost mechanized. Where there is a steady stream of men to exploit, the manager can reduce his recruiting effort to another version of the numbers game that insurance men are always playing. For example, the urban agency can rely almost entirely on advertising as a source of prospective salesmen.

SALES CAREER—Salary $400–$700 + com. Outstanding opty for highly motivated man who has owned his own business or served in mgmnt capacity either sales or administration.
SALES, PRUDENTIAL INSURANCE CO.—Immediate salary and training. $6,000–$9,000.
EXECUTIVE SALES POSITION—$750 per mo salary + comm 2 yr contract. We will train you (insurance). Coll or sales exp pfd. For a man of $10,000 yr calibre.

Any man who has ever looked for a job has seen advertisements like these in the Help Wanted columns. Such ads are run daily or weekly by the agencies of many different companies, and each insertion will bring in its share of responses. Once in a while some outfit will try what it thinks is a more sophisticated ad, like the following, which appeared in the business section of at least one Sunday paper in New York.

WANTED: Extremely intelligent, highly articulate, independent minded executive age 35–45. The man we're looking for must be successful, aggressive, willing to take direction but still and all very much his own kind of guy. We're specialists in developing such men into professionals in the fields of employee compensation, estate analysis, and business planning. If you think you qualify, call or write . . .

This gem wasn't meant to be spotted by an outsider as a life insurance recruiting ad.

In fact, about half the ads run by insurance agencies suppress the information that the job is an insurance-selling proposition. The idea is to tempt into the agency those men who normally wouldn't even dream of seeking such a job. Other managers explain that the job involves selling life insurance because "we only want repliers who know what it's all about." To a neutral observer, the results seem about the same either way. Besides, that *suppressio veri* is only a little white lie alongside the real lies the advertisements tell. And the mendacity of the ads is as nothing compared to the deceitfulness practiced in turn by the agency's recruiter once he gets a live candidate inside the door.

The recruiter leaves simple instructions in case anyone calls or writes in response to an ad: have the man come in. "Hell, we'll hire any warm body," one recruiter explained. "We don't want résumés, we don't want to exchange letters. We want to get our hands on the man, whoever he is." His philosophy could hardly be more explicit: he's in the business of *hiring*, not selecting, salesmen.

The first steps of the recruiting process are relaxed and seemingly informal. When the candidate arrives, he's shown into a comfortable office and given the usual employment-and-personal-history blank to fill out. Then he takes a test.

Even the most violent anti-test crusader would have to laugh at the test given to prospective life insurance salesmen.

True, this sales-aptitude test was designed by a recognized supplier for the Life Insurance Agency Management Association, and since its inception the test has been updated several times. But the test is meant to take little longer than forty-five minutes, and for anyone with even the mildest interest in becoming a life insurance salesman, it's almost impossible to give the wrong answers. (In at least one agency a friendly secretary is on hand to supply hints to candidates the manager particularly wants to hire.) Within moments after he finishes the test, someone tells the candidate that he did extraordinarily, amazingly well. In contrast to the seriousness with which these tests are given by most non-insurance employers, this situation is farcical.

Many home-office and trade-association experts claim to believe in these tests, and to them, the farce is naturally disturbing. Faced with the continuing need to add more salesmen, however, most agency managers put no faith whatever in tests or testing. Besides, even an effective test would be licked from the start. If necessary, the manager will falsify test results before putting them on the record of the man he may hire. "All we really want to know is whether the candidate can read," one assistant manager, not particularly cynical, commented.

But the real reason for these tests, as far as the manager is concerned, has nothing to do with screening out undesirables. Like everything else about recruiting, the test is only another stage in the process of persuasion. It's used to *sell the candidate* on the care and attention this company supposedly gives to picking salesmen.

Once the test is out of the way, the candidate is moved on to the next phase, a lengthy interview with the recruiter. Any real screening or selection is done here. As in a life insurance sales interview, the recruiter, who certainly must himself be a good salesman, will make sure his prospect is a normal individual, and not, for example, an obvious unemployable, a seasonal job-seeker, or an antisocial type. Beyond that, it's helpful if the candidate is (1) fairly presentable, (2) intelligent enough to learn something about insurance sales, and (3) in rather urgent need of a job. Aside from this last point, it seems as if almost any American can qualify for selling life insurance somewhere, just as almost any American can usually qualify for buying it.

Here, by the way, we can pinpoint the first lie told by the recruiting ad, which so often stipulates that a man must have previous sales, management, administrative, or other executive-level business experience. No such qualification is necessary; it's enough to have held down almost any job (or for that matter to have been jobless). The presumably more sophisticated agencies in the big cities give some preference to the white-collar candidate, and respectability is obviously an advantage. Mentioning all those "executive" posts in the ad is just another way to make insurance work seem attractive.

During this first interview the recruiter will attempt to learn something about the candidate's personality and general background. The interviewer may also begin to spell out the appealing reasons why the candidate should choose insurance sales as a career. But the real recruiting pitch can't begin until the agency staff learns a little more about the candidate, so this interview ends with a promise to "let the man know." The candidate leaves with a pocketful of literature about the joys of an insurance man's job; and there's a hiatus of several days in the recruiting process.

In this interim the candidate's statements about himself will be checked and his previous employment record confirmed ("investigated" is too strong a word; it's just the usual once-over-lightly credit report). Then the entire dossier will be scanned by management. The thoroughness with which this part of the process is conducted depends on company requirements, on the urgency of the manager's need for the candidate, and on how recently the agency has been stung by a fraudulent applicant.

As soon as the candidate's background is checked, the wheels begin to grind again. The candidate—if he hasn't changed his mind or found another job—is summoned back, this time for a series of shorter meetings with various members of the staff. In a small or new agency this procedure might involve one or at most two interviews. But in a better-established "shop" the candidate will make the rounds of a number of assistants before winding up in the manager's office.

In those agencies which have developed recruiting into a real art, the recruiter will have the candidate "drop in on" a successful salesman who "happens to be in the office" that day. The salesman will chat with the candidate and perhaps "tell him how things really are" in the life insurance business. (The salesman is there by prearrangement, and his "frank discussion" with the candidate sometimes comes out of a book.) If the candidate joins up, the salesman may earn a cash bonus or at least be in line for a case of whiskey or some theater tickets.

These interviews are designed to make the candidate feel at home, to impress him with the general air of prosperity and good spirit, and to disarm him of any skepticism he might feel about the job he's being wooed so hard to accept. Moreover, this "all-around-the-agency" pattern is meant to pique the candidate's curiosity and set up an atmosphere of expectancy. There must be something special about an industry which takes so many pains with prospective employees, the agency wants the candidate to think. Here I've been filling out forms, taking a test, being interviewed, and meeting executives in the best job-hunting tradition—except that *here* they've treated me as if I were important. The candidate probably won't notice that the warmth of this welcome is slightly impersonal and the agency's enthusiasm somewhat forced.

And he wouldn't be human if he weren't still curious about those promises in the recruiting ad: the generous starting salary, the training program, and the chance to progress into management.

So when he finds himself sitting in the manager's office, the candidate is usually still eager to find out what will happen next.

What does happen depends on what the manager has learned about him from written reports and his assistants' comments. The interview also depends on the manager's own favorite recruiting tactics, his personal acquaintance with the candidate (or the candidate's friends), and a whole host of other intangibles. Some managers don't even like to conduct this interview at the office. Like many other modern pitchmen, they prefer to do this part of their job over a luncheon table or at dinner.

The candidate will find himself listening to a velvet-smooth sales presentation conducted by an expert whose sincerity and conviction will be impressive. The virtues of life insurance, the rich rewards of a selling career, and the promise of an exciting future will all be spread before him; and the manager's favorite phrases to describe such delights will ring sweetly in his ears.

The shrewd manager won't attempt to hide the fact that the life insurance business has its drawbacks. But, the manager will always add, the problems of selling life insurance only serve to bring out a man's best qualities: perseverance, courage, industriousness, intelligence.

"Of the men I've recently met under these circumstances," one manager loves to say to his spellbound candidates, "it seems to me that you"—he pauses for emphasis—"may well have the most natural ability. And I really believe that together we can give you the opportunity to grow, to enhance your life, and in case you're not a charitable institution"— he smiles—"make you, frankly, richer than you ever dreamed you'd be. So how about it? Will you give us that chance?"

This particular manager is unusually fluent and imaginative. For the manager who doesn't trust his own persuasiveness, there are many texts to memorize. Selling the life insurance career has its own canned spiels, just as selling insurance does.

If the candidate finds the manager's rhetoric stirring, he may even sign a salesman's contract right on the spot. Some of the manager's promises may be a little vague, and some of the candidate's questions may go unanswered. But—so the candidate thinks—there's no reason why such details can't be straightened out later. The important thing for us to keep in mind is this: the candidate is probably out of a job and anxious for new employment; or the candidate may have been recommended to the agency by a friend or some person he has reason to trust. For one reason or another, the prospective life insurance salesman—unlike his more skeptical relative, the insurance customer—will very often want to believe the things he's being told.

So the new candidate agrees to come into the life insurance business. The recruiting stage is over, and the hiring stage begins. This consists of two simultaneous procedures: (1) the more or less mechanical activity of taking on a new recruit and (2) a certain amount of further psychological "preparation." To deal with the second matter first, the new agent must now be convinced that he's made a wise choice. Equally important, his wife must also be convinced, because life insurance is one business in which the salesman's wife can really make or break him. The long hours, endless demands, and possibility of economic strain all have to be made as palatable as possible.

The astute manager will hasten to make friends with the new employee's wife. The chances are that he'll invite the couple to dinner at an expensive restaurant and exert every ounce of his charm to convince her that the future will bring wonders for her and her family. At the same time, the manager will be sizing up the relationship between husband and wife, filing away in the back of his mind opinions about the lady's intelligence, taste, and willingness to co-operate. Many wives find such attention both obvious and distasteful, but that won't faze the manager.

One reason the Agency System regards this wifemanship with dead seriousness is that the wife, according to management folklore, sets the economic pace for the marriage. "We want a man who's frankly running a little bit scared," one manager states. "If the wife has expensive tastes and wants to live well, she'll push the man better than we can." And most managers also know that regardless of whether a man is succeeding or failing, a discontented wife can mean real trouble.

Becoming an insurance man also calls for other, more usual employment routines, such as passing a medical exam and moving into an office. And now, of course, is the time for the new recruit to be confronted by the question of money. What did that ad say about a salary?

"That's our special system of field compensation," the manager will smoothly explain. "Under this system a new man draws whatever salary he needs. So for the first three years—and if you want, even longer—you'll be taking home a regular pay check, with raises and bonuses based on your production. Now, I see you've been making five hundred dollars a month. Suppose we start you at six hundred . . ."

After this little speech the manager will slide across the

desk three copies of a contract. The recruit, still bemused by the casual way he's just been given a raise, will undoubtedly put his name on that contract as eagerly as a mouse puts his nose in the trap. Needless to add, he won't read a word of it; and even if he did, he wouldn't understand it.

He won't understand the all-important fact that the *company doesn't consider him an employee at all.* Small wonder. What better evidence of employment is there than a contract? The last thing our new man suspects is that *his* contract enlists him, legally speaking, in the ranks of the *self*-employed. And he certainly won't realize that as far as money is concerned, the manager's explanation tells something other than the truth, that his contract really spells out a system of getting paid that's as different from a salary as chalk is from cheese. The new recruit isn't getting a salary at all. Like every insurance salesman since the beginning, he's earning straight commissions.

Traditionally the insurance salesman (or "agent," as we should now begin to call him) has been awarded commissions on the assumption that he must be paid not only for selling life insurance but also for keeping the insurance in effect and up to date once it's sold. As soon as the customer pays his first year's premium charge, the agent is allowed a hefty first-year commission. Even in conservatively regulated New York State, this commission can run as high as 55 per cent of the annual premium. When the insurance owner pays his subsequent yearly premiums, the agent receives a more modest "renewal commission." Under the standard commission schedule, renewal commissions— which usually come to 5 per cent of the premium each time —are payable for a period of up to nine years. Thus, "fifty-five and nine fives" is the salesman's stock phrase for describing how he gets paid. It's no coincidence that this formula yields a total commission exactly equal to one year's premium.

With this commission schedule in mind, we can puzzle out the problem that the new recruit won't face until it's too late: How can a man supposedly paid only on a commission basis possibly receive a salary? The answer is he can't.

If we remember that there's a nation-wide shortage of salesmen and an even more desperate shortage of men willing to sell insurance, the whole situation makes better sense. For this means that in getting salesmen, the insurance industry must compete against businesses that not only pay salaries but offer generous fringe benefits as well. As we know, the life insurance industry doesn't believe in salaries for its salesmen (let alone paid vacations, sick leave, or anything else). The industry doesn't believe in *employing* salesmen in the first place. And yet, the companies do have to recruit somehow.

So within about the last ten years the Agency System has devised an ingenious way of "reconciling" the two opposites: the *commission* arrangement that the industry likes and the *salary* it despises but is forced to offer as bait.

This new method, which is in fact a supplement to the standard commission contract, goes by the name of the "validation agreement."

Superficially this agreement resembles the old-fashioned "drawing account" used in other commission-sales businesses. Under the usual drawing account, a salesman can request his employer to pay him a regular weekly or monthly sum out of the commissions he's earned. That way the salesman can make sure his money lasts between sales. Some employers will even let a man "get behind on his draw" and go into debt to the company if they expect the salesman to recover his financial health shortly. By and large, a drawing account is a helpful adjunct to commission earnings—at least for an experienced and money-wise salesman.

But the life insurance industry thrives on inexperienced and unsophisticated men.

So its validation agreement is advertised as a "salary," or even more dishonestly as a "salary plus commission," not as a version of the drawing account. Of all the lies recruiting ads tell, this one is the most flagrant. Many companies further the deception by calling their validation agreements "salary plans," and the recruiter will beguile the new candidate with the term "salary" until the contract is signed. Both the legal and the psychological point of no return has usually been passed before the new candidate discovers that his so-called salary is in fact no such thing and that his status as an employee is entirely illusory.

Two key points of the validation agreement make the new man's situation painfully clear:

(1) The agent must sell, within a given period, enough life insurance (and thus earn enough *commissions*) to justify, or "validate," the money advanced to him regularly as "salary." If the salesman doesn't make the grade, the "salary" stops. Then, in order to get paid at all, the man must switch to a straight-commission contract. If he gets far enough behind even before the given period is up, the manager has the authority to withhold the "salary" anyway, at least until the man makes up the difference.

(2) Under a validation agreement the agent relinquishes all legal rights to the commissions he earns. If he quits (to change companies, for example) or he's fired while he's ahead, he forfeits all of what he hasn't yet drawn. If he leaves while behind, he can't take a nickel with him, even if his renewal commissions will clearly exceed his actual indebtedness.

With a stick like this in his hand, the agency manager has every reason to believe that hiring and then controlling new salesmen will be easy. It must be admitted that along with the stick the manager can also manipulate the carrot. By adding bonuses or special "extras" to the commissions actually earned, the company can make some investment in the salesman; and most companies, however grudgingly, do so. However, such bonuses aren't paid directly to the man who earns them ("You think we're crazy?" one manager queried). Instead, they're thrown in with all that other money the salesman can't take with him if he leaves.

But most important, the business end of the validation agreement is a formidable bludgeon for the manager. After hooking his new man with a generous starting "salary," the manager can then keep the salesman under constant pressure until he's used up. Threatening to cut off the salesman's income is only the most obvious form of pressure. A manager who really knows the fine print in that validation agreement can easily develop such special kinds of leverage as arbitrarily *increasing* an agent's "salary" (a step that uses up credits already earned) and then working the man mercilessly to make him stay even. Another common variation of the basic theme is to "survive" a poor salesman if he happens to have good contacts. By a little fast shuffling of credits between salesmen's accounts, the manager can accomplish this at no cost to the agency. Once the manager has uncovered and exploited the victim's prospective customers, the man can be dumped unceremoniously.

True, the insurance company must protect itself against being sued by an agent or former agent whose manager is a bit light-fingered. But most companies don't really care what the manager does with the salesmen's validation accounts. They do penalize the manager if too many agents quit while they're far behind. But the truly resourceful manager *never* tells the indebted salesman that legally he has no obligation to pay back such arrears. Instead, when the agent leaves, the manager makes him sign a personal note for whatever is "owed." This the manager collects himself, and —since the company doesn't expect repayment—he quietly puts the money in his pocket.

To the untried salesman, justifying a "salary" beyond his reach can obviously become a nightmare. To have that contractual sword of Damocles hanging over his head does occasionally make an effective salesman out of a new man. But much more often, the fear of this sudden-death loss of income forces the beginner to sell insurance in ways that make even hardened veterans shudder. One man, for instance, found that the only way he could sell enough life insurance to validate his salary was to offer a rebate (i.e., a kickback) to his customers. Since rebating is a criminal offense in the state where he operated, every time this poor devil sold a policy he ran the risk of being turned in. He also ran the risk of being blackmailed by his customers. Sure enough, somebody did call his illegalities to the attention of the State Insurance Department. As a result, the man not only lost his agent's license and was fined enough money to bankrupt him, but was also sentenced to ninety days in the workhouse. (Mercifully the sentence was suspended.) He never did find out who informed against him. But his comrades in the agency knew that the informer was none other than the agency manager—who was disgruntled that the salesman wasn't kicking back enough to *him*.

Such utter rascality isn't necessarily the rule. But in almost every one of the thousands of life insurance agencies, salesmen are driven to commit fraud and near-fraud in order to keep on validating their so-called salaries. The agent who is under such pressure finds it temptingly simple to falsify his figures. He knows that his customers will never find out. For instance, he can quote a lower price than the policy actually costs, apologizing for his "error" later on. If the salesman is glib enough, you may willingly pay the few dollars' difference—forgetting that over the years the difference will cost hundreds of extra dollars. Or the agent may claim that "dividends will lower the premium substantially," knowing that you'll forget to check the actual dividends against his original projections. He may sell you a policy that pays *him* a higher commission—and costs *you* much more than you need to spend. And you'll never know; for just as he is at the mercy of his manager, so are you at his mercy.

Some insurance-company executives and even a few decent managers privately admit that despite its value as a recruiting gimmick, the validation agreement is nothing but a legalized fraud. "We'd be much better off telling the new guy what really lies ahead," one executive remarked. "Then at least he wouldn't hate life insurance when he failed." Yet this executive's company has one of the most deceitfully effective validation agreements in the industry. But you must realize that a big company sees its salesman in the same statistical terms in which it sees everything else. By fair means or foul, so many men are recruited, so many hired, so much insurance is sold, and so many men are terminated. Only the sales statistics really matter. The success or failure of the individual salesman means nothing whatever.

At this point the new salesman is feeling his way into a novel, unfamiliar, and grimly unique business environment: that of the life insurance agency. As our picture of what goes on at the agency level begins to take shape, one thing will be obvious. Given the manager's motives and requirements, plus the recruit's own needs and burdens, it's not surprising that a life insurance agency is a peculiar place. It's filled with people who shouldn't be there, and thus the scene of perpetual personal crisis.

"No matter what you do, most of these men will fail."
—*the Vice-President*

4 . *"Just Con Them a Little"*

MOST PEOPLE NEVER HAVE OCCASION to set foot inside a life insurance agency or to visit an agent at *his* office. Even if we did make such visits, our impression would more likely be one of bleak efficiency than of anything darkly satanic. Nevertheless, the assembly-line process of converting *people* into *insurance agents*—which this chapter explores in depth —is an unfunny parody of exactly what we might expect to find in an old-fashioned mill: creaky machinery, relentless pressure on the hired hands, and an appalling amount of failure.

Because the products of the Agency System's thousands of such mills are the men who sell us our life insurance, there's a special and highly personal reason for us to venture behind the scenes. If the insurance man is the victim of his own system, then every time we buy or even contemplate buying insurance, we become victims of the same system.

Our brand-new salesman will notice at once that half the desks in his agency are empty, many of its cubicles vacant. Everybody's out selling, his supervisor will quickly explain. "You can't make any money sitting at a desk" is Lesson No. 1 about being a life insurance man. The logic of that lesson will seem apparent, and later in the day the salesmen will begin to drift in and fill up some of that empty space. For quite a while the new man won't know just what most of these men really do with their time.

During his first few days on the job, the new man won't have much chance to think about anything he sees, because his own time will be as thoroughly programmed as that of a child in summer camp. The recruit's first efforts are divided between reading about insurance and being taught how to sell it.

So his morning hours are typically spent in classes, where, along with the other new men, he'll learn as much about insurance as the class supervisor, the agency, and the company want him to know. Teaching methods range from informal lectures and chalk-talks to elaborate audio-visual presentations. In recent years the entire life insurance industry has espoused the idea that "employee communications consultants" do a better job of sales training than the industry's own staff experts. Such outside firms lean heavily on films, recordings, and similar aids to enliven their "curriculum"; so life insurance men increasingly acquire their primary education from a movie projector. "It's certainly not the agent at one end of the bench and Mark Hopkins at the other," one serious-minded insurance educator remarked drily, when asked about the quality of this machine-teaching.

In essence, the new man is taught a somewhat more elaborate version of the factual material set forth in the first chapter of this book. But the emphasis is on the purely practical: how to compare one policy with another, how different forms of insurance can be tailored to fit a customer's real or imagined needs. At this point the Mandarin jargon of life insurance becomes the salesman's second language. He learns to think and speak in terms of "living values," "protection," and other euphemisms of sales promotion. Simultaneously the new agent picks up the technical vocabulary of his trade and begins to bore his wife with talk about "interest layback," "contingent beneficiaries," "dividend options," and similar quasi-professional gobbledegook. By the time he's finished his basic training, the new man won't know any other way to talk about his product.

Aside from his labors in the classroom, the recruit is given homework. On his very first day at the office he's handed a couple of thick, neatly indexed loose-leaf binders full of information about the company, its products, and the art of selling life insurance. He also receives what will become his Bible, the company's pocket-sized book of rates and technical information. For the two to three weeks that his basic training continues, the recruit's evenings at home will supposedly be spent in perusing this material, in completing written quizzes on insurance, and in learning how to use the ratebook.

The pages of that little book are covered with figures, and each set of figures tells a different story. A given company will provide sixty or seventy separate forms of life insurance for every age between zero and seventy. (Above seventy, rates must be obtained from the home office—along with special permission to sell the insurance.) The salesman who "knows his way around the ratebook" is thought to have an enormous advantage over a competitor who has trouble handling his own figures. Using that book, a brand-new man can work out the details of any given policy in about ten minutes. After a few months he'll be able to do it in seconds.

Unfortunately, the man who has mastered this purely mechanical chore is usually assumed to possess as much knowledge of the product as is necessary. The beginning of real insight into life insurance is a sense of the way simple laws underlie some very complex arithmetic, a feel for the mathematical logic that relates life, death, and money. But most new insurance men aren't encouraged to think in such terms at all.

The new man's training is more concerned with other matters. For example, the company's philosophy is sure to be spelled out in the first section of the salesman's training manual. The entire vast company organization, so the recruit is told, came into being in order to answer a great need and to serve the public. The company's management is likewise dedicated to this task. The basic requirements for success in the life insurance business are scrupulous honesty, hard work, and above all a selfless dedication to the service of the insurance-buying public. Testimonials, inspirational texts, and even Biblical quotations underscore the virtues of such success and conclude on an upbeat the new man's initial dose of assigned reading.

It's easy to laugh at this approach, especially in the light of what we already know about the life insurance business. But beginning insurance men naïvely do want to do good, and this fact provides management with powerful motivating and incentive-building opportunities. If the new salesman can be convinced, at least for a while, to take up his calling with missionary fervor, then training him presents fewer problems. The more idealistic a man is at the start, the easier it is for him to swallow the Agency System's basic, if insidious, rationale: *insurance is so beneficial that almost any means of selling it is entirely justifiable in the long run.*

As early as his seventh or eighth day in the business the recruit is handed a special notebook. "Open the book to the page headed Names of Relatives," the supervisor orders. "Now, there are fifty blank lines on that page. Some of you have small families, but everybody has at least fifteen or twenty relatives—cousins, brothers-in-law, uncles. Jot down their names."

The supervisor moves on rapidly to cover close friends, acquaintances, fraternity or lodge brothers, college classmates, business contacts, church groups—until the whole range of possible acquaintanceship has been covered. When the routine is completed, the new man almost always asks just what these names are for.

"We want you to sell every one of these names life insurance!" the supervisor replies enthusiastically. "Those names belong to people who need insurance and want insurance. Look at it this way: How would you feel if a friend of yours died suddenly and left his family without enough money to get along on, *and you hadn't spoken to your friend about life insurance?* What would you say to your friend's widow if she asked you, 'Joe, why didn't you make John buy insurance?' "

Nothing could demonstrate more clearly than such indoctrination what management really wants from the new salesman. The new man must himself be sold the idea that life insurance is a universal need. Having bought this concept, he can then be pressured into exploiting his own personal relationships for insurance purposes—as long as those relationships last.

To have the new man start with the inventory of people he knows best (and presumably has the best chance of selling to) is certainly the easiest way for management to make him productive. And the more friends and relations the new salesman can sell, the better—because it's a foregone conclusion that most of the recruits will ultimately fail. As far as getting the most out of them is concerned, the agency manager is trained to think in terms of weeks and months, not of years. So the salesman must be made to start with his own list of clay pigeons.

After filling up his notebook, the recruit is instructed to transfer all those names onto file cards and thereby systematize his stock of potential customers. He'll now have to remember his prospects' addresses, telephone numbers, and useful personal history. Which of his friends recently suffered a death in the family and is therefore in the right frame of mind to consider buying insurance? Who might be generous enough to throw a little business his way? As soon as this information-gathering has begun to yield a supply of names, and while the new man's self-confidence is at a peak, the recruit is ready for his moment of truth.

He must now attempt to sell his first life insurance policy.

For many men this very first sale is no real test, because some relative or friend makes things easy for the fledgling. "I hear you're in the life insurance business, Joe," goes the friend's kind-hearted speech. "Well, I do need some insurance and I'd like to help you out, so come on over and write me up a policy." This unbusinesslike event can happen often enough to postpone a recruit's real tribulations until after he's made a total commitment, emotional and financial, to the business.

As a rule, the new man's supervisor accompanies the recruit on such order-taking interviews and actually makes the sale while the recruit watches and listens to learn how it's done. Under the circumstances, selling life insurance seems like a cinch. But the time soon comes when the new insurance man runs out of obliging friends and relatives and has to begin dealing with less obliging ones. Against such a day, he has been trained to use other methods.

"Paul? This is Joe . . . Fine, thanks, and you? . . . Paul, as you may have heard, I'm now in the life insurance business, and while I have no reason to believe you're interested in adding to your program at this time, I do have access to certain ideas and information which may be of value . . ."

The recruit is sitting at his desk in the bull pen with a stack of his index cards in front of him. Propped up so he can read from it is a three-page printed folder entitled *Successful Telephone Techniques.* After a couple of hours' practice with his supervisor the new man is trying to use what he's learned, with his acquaintances as guinea pigs. Chances are that this is his first real selling effort; by now he's been in the life insurance business about ten days. The folder with his script printed on it is made of stiff cardboard. As the new agent—palms sweaty from nervousness—makes his calls and delivers his spiel, his voice sounds stiffer than that cardboard. But (if he follows the printed sales talk) not even the rawest recruit will discuss *insurance* over the telephone. "You can't sign up your prospect on the phone," reads the exhortation on the folder, "so forget about life insurance and sell the interview."

". . . Paul, it would only take about twenty minutes of your time to learn how these ideas would apply in your particular case. Could you give me the courtesy of that amount of time Tuesday afternoon at four, or would Wednesday morning be better?"

To render artificial phrases fluently requires the same diligence as learning to be a Shakespearean actor. Those agencies that take selling by telephone seriously conduct actual seminars in technique. "Be Natural!" one booklet on the subject exhorts. "You can put a smile in your voice if you put a smile on your face. So relax, think of something pleasant, and let that broad smile appear."

The sight of a room full of salesmen, each one talking into the telephone with a wide smile on his face, can be disquieting, to say the least. And when the party at the other end of the line begins to make things difficult, it can be hard to keep that smile pinned securely in place.

"Well, I certainly can understand your being busy at this time of year, Paul. But my ideas won't take up more than a few minutes..." or,

"Well, frankly, if you told me you *were* interested in life insurance, I'd faint dead away." (Chuckle) "But my ideas and information could be of value to you in case you ever contemplate a future purchase..." or,

"Paul, just about everybody has a brother-in-law in the business, but maybe my ideas and information can show you how to make your present insurance more valuable..."

The above, of course, are the printed answers to three of the most common objections the solicitor hears: (1) too busy, (2) not interested, and (3) a relative in the business. In every case, the salesman is supposed to answer the objections by asking once again for a definite appointment. "Statistics prove," that folder states, "that most interviews aren't granted until the request is made four times."

"Well, look, Paul. I plan to be in the neighborhood on Tuesday anyway. Suppose I stop by and spend a couple of minutes with you, just to shake your hand." If this doesn't work, nothing will, and the recruit is instructed not to try any further. (The experienced man rarely prolongs his efforts this far.)

By the time this first telephone session is over, the recruit is usually exhausted both physically and emotionally. But he'll have learned something about the realities of insurance that nobody will have told him before: it's tough to make a sale.

For many a new man, alarm replaces self-confidence after he calls the first half-dozen friends to tell them the glad tidings of his new career—and finds them a good deal less friendly than he'd expected. This is the recruit's first exposure to "insurance agent's syndrome," a roller-coaster alternation between moods of optimism ("My cousin was a push-over") and fits of depression ("I can't get an appointment to save my life"). A single half hour on the telephone is usually more than the beginner can stand. After such a session some recruits flatly refuse to do any more telephoning at all that day. But most new men take comfort in the cheery words of the supervisor. "You had nine turndowns in a row? Well, you're only one more no away from a yes!" The supervisor knows that the recruit must develop a reasonably good telephone manner—as well as weather this first experience of rejection.

So the shrewd unit manager sits in the bull pen with his recruits while they make their calls. He jokes about the answers they're getting, rejoices at a success, analyzes why a man is having trouble ("Slow down, Joe, and *smile*, smile until your face cracks"). He'll make the whole nerve-racking ordeal as much like a game as possible, running contests between recruits, buying coffee, letting the men take frequent short breaks. As with anything else, there's an art to running a successful bucket shop—and that, of course, is exactly what this is. Gradually the jolt of rejection will trouble the recruit less, and this plus a little success in getting appointments will restore some of his self-assurance. After a week or two the recruit will doggedly work on the telephone for several hours a day. But no insurance man ever *likes* telephoning, and some men develop reactions which are positively neurotic. For instance, after a particularly grueling afternoon —seventy-six calls, zero appointments—one rookie tore his telephone loose from its connections and flung it at the supervisor. "Then," this former agent remarked with gusto, "I went out and got stoned."

As he spends more time on the telephone the recruit learns that his supply of friends, relatives, and acquaintances won't last forever; the logistics of telephone solicitation see to that. A persistent man can make fifteen to twenty telephone contacts per hour. About one third of the people he's trying to reach will for one reason or another be unavailable; so he'll actually talk to ten to fourteen people. If he makes even one appointment, he's lucky. Four or five hours on the telephone will use up sixty to eighty names; and therefore, even the friendliest recruit soon begins to run out of people to call. So even while he's still sifting through his circle of acquaintances, management has begun to drill him in other ways of finding prospective customers, such as begging for prospects, as well as sales, from the people he already knows.

"George, let me ask you a question. Suppose there were a way you could guarantee income at retirement to a friend of yours, or guarantee your friend's son a college education —without its costing you a cent. You'd do it, wouldn't you? ... Well, all you have to do is introduce me to three of your friends . . ."

First the salesman sells an interview. Then he tries mightily to sell insurance. And finally, whether or not he succeeds at his primary task, the salesman is supposed to sell his customer the idea of referring him to others. This is the standard Agency System method of training the salesman to keep himself in circulation.

Ideally such a "referred lead" system should work wonders for the salesman because the system enables him to call only on people who know in advance who he is and what he's selling. The salesman who conscientiously asks to be referred to new prospects should never run out of people to see. But in practice, this "endless chain" technique rarely works for the new man.

People may be willing to buy their own life insurance from the new salesman, but most people are understandably reluctant to turn a life insurance agent loose on their friends, and an inexperienced agent at that. It's not as if insurance men were hard to come by—so the usual reasoning goes—and besides, sending an insurance man to a friend is a little bit like sending him a present of soap: an unfriendly reminder.

Nevertheless, in training agents, the manager and his associates still put great stress on endless-chain prospecting and getting referred leads. The reason is obvious: such methods are easy to teach and cost next to nothing. Moreover, these strategies require no special marketing knowledge on the supervisor's part and demand no insight into the individual agent's qualities and capabilities.

Thus, once he uses up his supply of personal contacts and finds that referrals are hard to come by, the agent realizes that as far as seeking new customers is concerned, he's very much on his own. His discovery of this fact may coincide with the discovery that he's on his own in most other ways, too. Management has furnished him with minimal facilities for learning about life insurance. His agency has provided rudimentary training in how to sell. The recruit has a desk, a mailing address, a telephone—but nothing more. In return, management has gained the new man's willing cooperation in knocking down a few easy birds. Those three or four sales to friends and relatives have already more than repaid the expenses of the company's "investment."

And thus, in three weeks to a month the honeymoon is over.

At this point decent management men may sympathize with the not-quite-so-new salesman. The new man's immediate supervisor may now explain, or try to explain, the rationale underlying recruitment, hiring, and training. But the moment has come when the agent must be told that he's got to look after himself. Besides, by this time there's a newer crop of recruits to process, and there isn't much a busy supervisor can do for this month-old veteran.

No wonder one company vice-president sums up the new agent's predicament by stating flatly that "between the first and the sixth month a new man's survival is largely a matter of luck." It takes something special to withstand the rigors of selling life insurance. The unconcern of the management about the given agent's sales success adds another load to his burden. And the agent who does survive learns that at this stage, success consists of a series of tiny triumphs and slender prizes.

Thus, it's a victory to steal or charm an interoffice telephone directory from a receptionist because a company phonebook is a good source of names. When he begins to pull other names from the society or business columns of the daily papers, the new man tests himself in competition with dozens of other salesmen. Wedding, engagement, birth (and death) announcements and reports of job promotions or changes are the common gleaning ground of a community's new insurance men. If you get married, switch jobs, buy a house, or have a baby and you've been unwary enough to make the fact public, you'll be a target for every hungry agent in town.

For the new salesman, every telephone call is an exercise in self-discipline. Every interview is a cause for celebration. And every policy sold is a do-or-die effort, often for only the most modest cash return. At the best of times, to deliver the sales message in the necessary relaxed style is a challenge. To do so while full of worry about that validation agreement is almost impossible. And yet, customers don't want to talk about life insurance with a desperate salesman.

Those who survive during this initial period attribute their success in large part to one thing: outside economic resources. "I didn't inherit any trust fund," one now established agent commented, "but my wife was working, thank God, or we'd have starved."

But in the life insurance business, survival tactics depend on more than luck, extra income, or the ability to conceal insecurity behind the salesman's mask of perennial assurance. In *The Organization Man,* William Whyte recollects an old-fashioned sales manager who said to a group of budding salesmen, "Always remember that the man on the other side of the counter is your *enemy!*" At this point in his career the life insurance man forgets about the niceties and learns to channel his frustration, fear, and anger into effective salesmanship. After I'm established, he tell himself, I can afford to be a public benefactor.

Gradually he masters the art of making contacts. Where half an hour of telephoning once left him limp, the salesman can now make phone calls all day long. However, in learning how to use the telephone efficiently, he again finds himself up against a problem in logistics. "I spend so much time on the telephone," said one salesman plaintively, "that I don't have time to see the people I'm calling." If it sometimes takes four hours of telephoning to produce a single interview, the salesman has to work a forty-hour week simply in order to go to work. As a way out, the agent will very likely turn to an even more mechanical way of securing prospects: direct mail. This in turn entails drudgery of a very different kind because it's up to the agent to supply himself with mailing lists and do (or pay to have done) the coolie labor of addressing and mailing out his literature.

Nevertheless, most salesmen eventually do send out letters, purportedly from the company's executive offices, which not only offer insurance information but promise a free gift— anything from a memo pad to a road atlas—if the recipient returns a reply card. Except that too many who reply are interested only in the memo pad and not in life insurance, such mailing pieces do provide a steady, automatic way of prospecting for customers. The really hard-boiled agents dispense with such frills as free gifts and send out the cheapest, crudest form of direct mail they can buy. "I'm not in the memo pad business," one agent observed tartly.

Even the most desperate life insurance salesman avoids door-to-door canvassing like the plague. "What do you think I am," he'll demand if his supervisor suggests such last-ditch methods, "an encyclopedia salesman?" However, there are times when a man will do anything. "We used to go into those tenements, stand in the hallways, and yell 'Seguros'— Spanish for *insurance*. If anybody stuck his head out the door and hollered 'Sí!' we'd climb the stairs and make our pitch. Until the company made us quit, we were making six or seven sales a day that way." Such methods may seem out of date, to put it mildly. But this agent was merely describing what he did to sell life insurance in New York's *barrio*, or Puerto Rican ghetto, in 1961—and salesmen go through similar routines every day all over the country. You can imagine what it meant to this agent—a college graduate with years of business experience behind him—to have to peddle his wares in the slums.

The rare individual who can thus drive himself past humiliation stands a good chance of growing into an effective operator—as in fact the "Seguros" agent has done. Out of necessity such a salesman will learn how to cajole some customers and bully others. But he'll also learn how to be convincing. Gradually the numbers of sales he makes will increase; and after one year, or two, or three, the agent will find himself meeting the quota and perhaps even justifying his starting "salary." After five years (or longer), he'll still be working a sixty-hour week and he'll still be out most nights and week ends. The salesman will have adjusted his personal habits accordingly, as part of the job—in short, he will have survived. But while the threat of outright failure haunts him less, success continues to recede before him like a mirage.

According to an authoritative agent training manual, "The average successful salesman of life insurance . . . earns $4,000 a year in first-year commissions." Taking into account renewal commissions and extra allowances, this means that such a salesman will eventually reach an average level of income of $7,500 to $8,000 a year, with a maximum (after about twenty years) of $10,000. It's no coincidence that once a salesman reaches this $4,000-a-year commission mark, many companies admit him to "production clubs," paying his way to conventions, and the like. Agents making this kind of money after ten, fifteen, or twenty years of hard labor are the stalwarts on whom the industry and the public depend. But to many of us, an insurance man's "average success" will seem like little more than bare subsistence.

The grim vocational truth about the insurance agent's calling is that survival is no guarantee of success. On the contrary, the Agency System's version of a career more nearly resembles a treadmill. If a man does keep his balance climbing on, he then gets a chance to go on running in the same place forever.

The crowning irony is that the very methods the agent must use in order to survive are almost certain to block him from achieving any real success, as most of us understand

71·

the term. For the insurance man who does drag himself up to that average-successful level can almost never acquire the knowledge and background necessary to sell insurance on a really substantial scale. His earnings will be based on the sale of small or medium-sized policies to small or medium-sized customers. And in order to maintain those earnings, the average-successful agent must work unceasingly at the thing he knows, pushing life insurance. So he has little time or energy left with which to dig into the complexities of a business world outside his daily routine, and his *savoir-faire* will never be equal to dealing with really important customers.

Persuading the sharp-eyed executives, lawyers, and accountants who make insurance decisions not only for themselves but also for their well-heeled clients demands something more than persistence and will power. To work with such sophisticated buyers requires detailed, specialized knowledge. Any insurance man who aspires to the most lucrative market for his product must know tax and commercial law, business analysis, and economics. He must, of course, be supremely versed in the intricacies of insurance itself. Finally, this salesman must be able to socialize and conduct easy business relationships with the people he wants to make his customers. This means behaving superbly in the soft-spoken role of the consultant, and exuding professional authority and objectivity. How many life insurance agents can meet such standards?

In recent years an organization called the Million Dollar Round Table has obligingly made public the results of a continuing survey of its membership. As the name implies, the MDRT is composed of men who regularly sell $1,000,000 worth of life insurance or more a year. In fact, according to an MDRT brochure, "The Million Dollar Round Table is one of the most exclusive 'clubs' in the world . . . comprising only about *one percent* of all life insurance agents!" The organization's 1965 survey drew answers from 2,000 of its 4,500 members, which should place its statistical accuracy beyond question. And up to a point the statistics of success do speak for themselves.

Among these leading salesmen, the annual income averages about $29,000 and ranges from under $10,000 to over $150,000. About two thirds of the MDRT's members earn between $11,000 and $40,000 a year; another 23 per cent earn between $40,000 and $75,000; and 10 per cent earn over $75,000. Even allowing for the fact that in some cases a good deal of this income is derived from non-insurance sources, the million-dollar salesmen make good money at their trade. And from additional information in the survey, it's apparent that these salesmen operate in ways that have little to do with standard Agency System training. For instance, the average MDRT member makes fewer than twenty phone calls a *week* for interviews. Yet the MDRT agent sees 20 per cent *more* prospects than the average man, and he sells fifty to seventy-five policies a year, a very high average.

Such statistics do appear impressive; and they prove that despite the Agency System, some men at least can make a real career out of selling life insurance. "Why, these men are outstanding individuals," was the reaction of one guest at a special MDRT convention. "They're not like life insurance salesmen at all!"

But that remark merely drives home one absolutely crucial point. The true significance of the foregoing statistics, and indeed of the Million Dollar Round Table itself, is that in the life insurance industry only a disgracefully small handful of agents ever reach the top. (Moreover, we should note, this *crème de la crème* aren't as rich as all that. To be sure, the $29,000 average yearly income is eminently respectable, but not so startlingly high in an era when in other businesses hundreds of thousands of men, not just the top handful, do equally well.)

To the consumer, yet another point is equally crucial. The best men whom this industry's survival-of-the-fittest methods produce are a small group of prosperous salesmen plus perhaps another small cluster of competent men who never quite enter that charmed million-dollar circle. Beyond that, we have the thousands upon thousands of average-successful agents.

And so, in life insurance most people, if they're served in any meaningful fashion at all, are served by men who don't even come close to being successful in their own right.

What this really means to us as individuals is a subject reserved for full discussion later on. But here we can at least sense the nature of the problem. If the product in question were some tangible item—an appliance, a car, or even a house—most of us wouldn't care or ever need to care about the economic well-being of the man who sells it to us. If the dishwasher breaks, the car refuses to run, or the roof springs a leak, we have easy recourse to people who can straighten things out. But who fixes stupidly, incompetently, or dishonestly arranged life insurance?

According to the industry and the Agency System, we must look to the insurance man as the expert. To ourselves and our families, the agent is presented as an ex officio financial consultant who is especially reliable in case of an emergency. "The New York Life agent in your community is a good man to know," we read in one magazine ad. A competitor suggests, "Don't answer until you've talked with your Prudential agent, a 'real pro.'" But what kind of help or advice can we expect from someone who was hired in the first place because "he was running a little bit scared"? How trustworthy about our most intimate financial problems can any man be when his own financial future depends on making us buy something *right now?*

The statistics of success only remind us that as insurance buyers, millions of us must settle for the exact opposite of success. Indeed, every time the life insurance industry points with self-satisfaction to its "exclusive club," the MDRT, most insurance buyers have every right to be angry. Because a successful agent is so hard to find, we can conclude that the American Agency System has a great deal to answer for.

To understand how much trouble this system really causes, we should proceed to examine as best we can certain other much less accurate statistics. For there are figures that agencies do their best to hide from their parent companies, figures which these companies in turn conceal from their own top managements and from their competitors, figures that the industry shrouds in deep secrecy.

These, of course, are the statistics of failure.

Up to now, we have been filling in the portrait of an industry that sustains itself, and indeed thrives, on every single degree of unsuccess. Yet even though we may fully expect the worst, the ugly facts of failure in the life insurance business will still come as a shock. Of the approximately 110,000 men and women recruited, hired, and trained *each year* to sell life insurance, some 90,000—nearly 90 per cent—leave the business *within ninety days.* And by the end of each full year, year after year, another 5,000 to 10,000 have failed.

True, these aren't the figures that circulate within the industry. According to official sources, the "turnover ratio" among salesmen is much lower. Some of these sources estimate the ninety-day turnover rate as 65 per cent, and *The*

New York Times (in a 1965 article on tests for new recruits) cited surveys that give this rate 50 per cent. But with salesman turnover as with much else, this industry's officialdom demonstrates a remarkable capacity to minimize problems. Company sales executives are well aware that their agency managers falsify personnel records (for instance, by keeping agents' contracts on the books long after the men themselves have vanished from the scene). Companies themselves are anxious to whitewash their hiring and firing records. "We certainly don't feel that this is anything the public needs to know about," one high official said.

But whatever the exact percentages are, it's absurd to quibble about the statistics of disaster. For failure still overtakes the huge majority of those who enter the life insurance business. Even if the men who failed were few in number or of low calibre, such high *percentages* would be cause for bitter concern. But an appalling fact about this turnover is that so many of the men who fail are decent, enthusiastic recruits, not drifters or white-collar bums.

These fearsome statistics can't reflect the individual experience of failure, misery, and defeat a man tastes—often weeks or months before management actually intervenes— when he realizes that his efforts aren't going to make him successful. Theorizing about failure is a favorite hobby at every level of the industry, but no serious research has been done to learn why agents fail. The reason isn't far to seek. Nobody really cares to know.

"Most men fail because they don't do the automatic things. They don't send out mail, they don't telephone, they don't sell to their friends, so naturally they don't stay in the business." This is the agency manager speaking. To him, the recruit fails because he doesn't do the mechanics of the job, and superficially, of course, he may be correct. But most managers are also well aware that some sort of emotional disturbance (a disturbance of which the salesman himself may be completely unaware) underlies this reluctance to perform. But the manager's *own* training manuals preach the usual nonsense about "motivating" men with pep talks and certainly don't tell him anything worth knowing about why a man's energy and spirit may suddenly flag.

It's a pretty sure bet that the manager has himself been a fairly successful salesman and has the successful businessman's contempt for bad performance. Furthermore, somewhere along the line most managers have devoted hours of time, counsel, and personal help to agents who have thwarted their efforts by failing anyway. A few such experiences can harden even a compassionate manager's heart and beckon him to guard his psyche by hiring new recruits instead of sweating out the salvation of the old.

So for the most part, agency managers are content to talk about failure in the stale, old-fashioned, black-and-white terms that other businesses have long since discarded. "George has everything it takes to succeed. Trouble is, he's lazy. Joe over there could make it, too. But he's yellow, scared the customer will turn him down." Even those managers who presumably know better are still quick to identify laziness and cowardice as the *primary* causes of failure.

If we took these managers seriously, we would have to believe that every year 90,000 to 100,000 men drop out of life insurance business because they lack industry or are afraid. You can't find many executives willing to pass such contemptuous—and false—judgment on men they had courted assiduously a few months before.

Now let's turn to the companies themselves, where computers digest the sad facts of failure and spew them out as unemotional statistics. Here, high-level executives view the turnover figures with professional unease and—so they tell one another—work hard on ideas to improve matters. Significantly, however, their grand schemes are almost always aimed at recruiting *more* agents, so that the turnover problem won't ever affect sales. Any uneasiness these executives do feel is only that of businessmen whose methods aren't working as well as they should (though some of these executives act like men who definitely don't like being reminded of what their methods really produce).

For example, consider the reaction of one extremely able management official. As dispassionate as he usually is, this gentleman waxed at first argumentative and then irate on the subjects of recruiting and turnover.

"Look here," he said finally. "As an occupation, selling is held in low esteem in our society. And among all the sales categories—heavy equipment, food, and so on—life insurance selling is well down the list. This means there are only a limited number of men we can attract to our sales jobs.

"Whether we use fair means or foul, out of all the men we do attract a small percentage is going to beat our system and make a pot of money. As for the rest, it doesn't matter a damn *what* you do, pay them a real salary, double their commissions, or serve them breakfast in bed. They're going to fail."

In one form or another, these sentiments are echoed by dozens of executives throughout the industry. "We're sucking hind teat in the job market, and that's all there is to it," one official explained. His counterpart in another home office rephrased things a bit more elegantly: "It takes a special combination of skills to sell life insurance. Only a few men have these skills, so we're always going to have the problem of failure."

Yet despite their firm—and curiously, almost pleasurable

—conviction that endemic failure has to be the salesman's lot, some of these executives are also defensive about the problem. "Why pick on us?" is one of their favorite questions. The same executive who was quoted at length above was very eager to point out that other direct-sales industries (whose products range from encyclopedias to home improvements) have equally bad or even worse turnover records. In fact, according to this official, the life insurance industry is in pretty good shape by comparison.

But that other businesses practice equally unscrupulous tricks on the men they hire or display equally regrettable turnover ratios doesn't excuse the life insurance industry. Telling lies, offering phony security, and causing human wastage is vilely wrong. The life insurance business has no right to defend its dubious methods on the grounds that other enterprises do worse. On the contrary, this industry claims that its dedicated agents stand sleepless guard over the financial security of millions of Americans. That's enough of a reason why life insurance men should be immeasurably better-trained, more capable, and more secure than the men who offer, say, vacuum cleaners, cosmetics, or aluminum siding to the public.

In the end, most insurance executives shrug aside such charges, and defensive or not, justify the Agency System on the grounds of past successes and present expediency. As bad as they are, we're advised, the industry's sales methods have worked for seventy-five years. Today the public endorses the Agency System by the most direct means of all: buying billions of dollars' worth of insurance a month from its representatives. It's a pity—so goes the industry's refrain —that any large-scale distribution system must involve such waste of time, money, and human resources. But that's part of the price you must and will pay to have life insurance.

Year by year, millions of us buy life insurance from agents who won't even be around long enough to send their customers the insurance man's obligatory Christmas card. It's a stock joke in any life insurance agency that the average customer buys insurance seven times—from seven different agents. And that insurance men themselves think such gallows humor is funny speaks volumes about the quality of the service we can expect from the men who sell us our insurance.

Even the uncommon man who prides himself on the skill and thoughtfulness of his own agent pays a ransom each year to the Agency System. As that good agent is the first to admit, *somebody* has to pick up the tab for so much failure. Somebody has to pay for the dropout salesman and the high cost of distribution. That somebody, of course, is the public. We should expect to pay for the privilege of dealing with a specialist about a matter as personal and important as our life insurance. But must our contributions support instead an agent we can't trust and a system most of us would gladly change if we could?

Apparently so. At present the Agency System is still for most Americans the only game in town. But (as we'll be discovering in the next chapters) for many of us the range of choice is beginning to widen. A partial solution to the evils of the Agency System is already being written in various government offices, in the headquarters of huge pension and welfare funds, in corporation insurance departments, in banking and investment centers, and ironically, in many divisions of the life insurance industry. Even though this system continues to hold its sway over life insurance, its time may be running out.

"Don't sell any niggers life insurance."
—*the Manager, on underwriting*

5 . *Underwriting: Selection or Discrimination?*

BECAUSE SO MANY MILLIONS of people own insurance, you may automatically assume that you, too, will be able to get it when the time comes. And because you're begged over and over to buy, you may forget that somebody else (or rather a group of somebodies) really makes the decision about whether you *can* buy it or not. It may come as a shock to be reminded that insurance always involves a process of selection called "underwriting."

From the moment your agent tucks your application into his briefcase, you cease to be a person as far as the life insurance industry is concerned. To the agent, you are now a "case" for his agency to list on its records. Once the wheels of the underwriting process really begin to turn, you will be a parcel of statistics, to be considered in the same cold light as millions of other parcels are. In the impersonal but evocative language of those who will weigh your suitability for life insurance, you'll be known simply as a "risk."

The fact that you're called by this name is laden with significance. Logically, the risk in life insurance should be the amount of money that the company risks if it insures you, and insurance men do use the term "risk" in that sense. But in an extension of meaning that would do credit to a poet, the industry's technicians also use the word to indicate that the company's financial risk is in turn measured by the hazards to which your own life is daily exposed. Thus, in life insurance *you* are the "risk."

Not everybody is what a life insurance company considers a prime risk; i.e., someone eminently suitable for insuring. As far as the company that insures you is concerned, you may be less of a bargain than you imagine, for many reasons— some obvious, some puzzling, and some deeply disturbing.

Though you may not be fully aware of the fact, evaluation of your potential as a life insurance risk begins right in your living room—or kitchen. Aside from wanting to give your salesman a little prestige, there's a valid reason why the insurance company calls him by the title of "field underwriter." In insurance an underwriter is the man who selects and evaluates individual risks; and your agent is charged not only with persuading you to buy but also with collecting the basic information the company needs to decide about insuring you. Because this gathering of data requires a certain amount of on-the-spot judgment, your agent is an important contributor to the selection process.

When you fill out the application, you give your insurance man much more information than he needs for his own personal files. Besides the usual "vital statistics"—name, address, date of birth, and so on—the agent will question you about your past addresses and your employment history, going back at least five years. He'll also determine how much insurance you already own and whether any insurance company has previously turned you down. He'll ask whether you travel a great deal or take part in any other hazardous activities. In completing the application for at least one company, an agent will even have to ask whether you "presently engage in or contemplate engaging in (a) free-fall parachute-jumping or (b) skin-diving below the level of 50 feet."

This questionnaire is only the starting point for the company's research into your insurability, and the information *you* volunteer is by no means all of the information *the agent* passes on to his company. On the back of your application there's a special section for the "field underwriter" (or salesman) to complete. This section is for particularly personal information which the company knows most people don't want to supply openly. For instance, the agent must put down his estimates of your monthly income (from all sources); your net worth, or assets minus liabilities; whether you own or rent your home; and your wife's financial status. As we saw in the first chapter, the agent is something of an expert at sizing you up financially and finding out unobtrusively about such private matters as your debts, your investments, and your hopes for the future. He uses this fact-finding skill not only to sell you insurance but also to inform his home office about your ability to pay for it.

On the back of the application the agent must further indicate your status as a United States citizen, and if you are one, whether by birth or naturalization. If you were naturalized, he must determine the dates of your entry into the United States and the conferment of your citizenship. If you're neither a citizen nor a prospective citizen, most American companies refuse to insure you. The official explanation is that an alien, unless permanently residing in this country or Canada, is likely to return to his native land. There, the hazards confronting him may be greater and the insurance company may find it harder to do business. An underwriter in the Bronx may well be unfamiliar with conditions in

Buenos Aires or Bangkok. But one selection expert phrased his company's reasons much more crisply: "Foreigners make us nervous."

The company also wants to know what race you belong to, and not out of idle curiosity or "for identification purposes" or "because we collect statistics" (which is what one sales executive tells his agents to say if anybody gets curious about the back of that application). In some states questions about race are outlawed from insurance applications. In New York, for instance, the agent who wants to keep in the good graces of his company's Selection Department has to figure out a way of tipping off the home office in case you happen to be Negro, Oriental, or "of Spanish or Latin American extraction." The new recruit in particular will be reminded about answering this question and blandly cautioned to "complete the entire application."

Besides responding to such bluntly specific queries as those about race and finances, the field underwriter will be asked to "give his opinion of the character and reliability of the applicant," including "any information, favorable or unfavorable, which might have bearing on the company's decision." In theory, the company is entirely justified in asking the salesman for his opinion. The home-office specialists never lay eyes on you, and a few pertinent sentences from the one man who does have first-hand knowledge could be very helpful. The successful agent knows that such helpfulness makes it easier for him to "sell the risk to the Selection Department," that accurate information pays off.

But most agents, your own man probably included, can remember only one thing: if the customer doesn't qualify for insurance, the salesman doesn't make any money. So the run-of-the-mill salesman rarely tells the selection experts anything unfavorable. His evaluation is usually cursory, if not actually tainted with overoptimism. "I'll swear the agent thinks 'net worth' is the same thing as 'total installment debt,'" one veteran home-office underwriter mutters. "At least, that's what it looks like when we get the whole story." From this more or less official reaction, we can rightly deduce that the Selection Department's faith in the field underwriter is limited.

Home-office underwriting specialists, however, have access to less biased sources of information. The company operates under the theory that if the agent knows the Selection Department conducts its own investigations, he will be more honest in evaluating his applicants. But a certain amount of tension always builds up between the professionally optimistic salesman and the professionally mistrustful home-office underwriters. The agent, who goes through such agonies merely in order to sign you up, naturally wants the company to certify you as a Grade A risk and issue you a policy accordingly. The selection experts, being company men, must operate under stricter rules. To check and to enlarge on what the agent uncovers, the Selection Department makes use of outside inspections. These usually routine investigations are performed by such firms as Retail Credit, Inc., of Baltimore. The inspector (often a retired police detective or a college student working part-time) will probably telephone the local bank to check your account and the county clerk's office to ask whether any judgments are outstanding against you. More important, he'll visit your neighborhood, ring a few doorbells, and quiz your neighbors about your living habits. Are you quiet and well behaved? Do you drink or use alcoholic beverages to excess, throw wild parties, and in general lead a high life?

If you plan to buy a large amount of insurance, $50,000 worth or more, the inspection will be far more searching and much more professionally carried out. Because the company will have so much at stake, its own expert and experienced special investigators will handle your case. The home-office staff inspector is trained to uncover and analyze the details of even the most obscure or complicated personal background and to handle his inquiry with the delicate touch of a diplomat. An ace inspector can put together your dossier without your ever becoming aware of what's going on—though in most cases he'll make a special point of contacting you personally so that you'll understand and co-operate.

In ninety-nine cases out of a hundred, even routine investigations are conducted with care, discretion, and reasonable accuracy. But the sheer number of investigations now being made almost guarantees that mistakes will happen. Typically, trouble starts when the inspector gets a real earful about you from a jealous or angry neighbor and blows your case wide open by basing his report on this "information." Or a problem arises because an inspector mistakes you for a notorious local alcoholic, reckless driver, or wife-beater. Usually somebody in the Selection Department spots the error in time to avoid mortal insult and injury, and you never find out how close you came to being rejected as a bad moral or financial risk.

But there are occasions when things don't turn out so well. Take the case of one gentleman who urgently needed to insure his life for $100,000. It seems his wife wouldn't grant him a divorce unless he obtained such a policy in favor of their daughter, a step which the man in question was entirely willing to take. He duly applied for the insurance, passed his medical checkup, and waited, only to be informed by the embarrassed agent that the company had declined him as a "poor moral risk."

All the man had done was move a few things into the apartment of the girl he was planning to marry as soon as his divorce became final. But this was enough for the insurance investigator to fix things so that he would be declined for insurance, his divorce wouldn't be granted, and he couldn't remarry and remove this moral stigma. For a long time the Selection Department absolutely refused to break the Kafkaesque circle. Not until reams of written explanation and character references had been submitted did the company consent to grant the insurance—and even then the company wanted to charge an extra price.

Similar stories are legion; every agent and home-office underwriter has a supply. But such mischances seldom befall the usual insurance applicant. You, for example, are undoubtedly a sober, industrious, solid citizen, and even if you're not quite so saintly, you still needn't worry. Unless your personal and financial habits make you a real menace, you can probably get life insurance as long as you're in good health.

There's a good deal that the Selection Department wants to know about your health status, past and present. Here the experts rely on the medical information furnished by an official company doctor (who may be a young resident supplementing his hospital income or a veteran of 10,000 insurance exams). Like the application, the medical-exam questionnaire is a basic source of information and a starting point for further investigation.

Sometimes the agent himself, and not a doctor, can ask you whether you've had ". . . goiter, cancer, tumor, cyst, growth, or syphilis"—or any other ailment. This "nonmedical" (no actual examination required) insurance is, among other things, a perfect example of how a life insurance company thinks in terms of numbers. How can a layman be entrusted with the professional's job of ascertaining your medical history?

Once, people who had recently bought life insurance were

known to be much healthier than the general population. But in recent years the gap between the "select" and the "general" mortality rates has been narrowing, which is an actuary's way of saying that *all* people are steadily growing healthier (and thus longer-lived) by insurance-company standards. As far back as the 1920's, some life insurance companies reviewed what was then only a trend in this direction and came up with the following:

(1) Every insurance medical exam costs the company money —the doctor's fee.

(2) If there were a way to offer life insurance without a medical exam, the company would save all those fees.

(3) True, without the professional scrutiny of doctors, the company would be allowing some poorer health risks to buy insurance, so the death rate among policy owners would go up.

(4) But the increased cost resulting from the extra death claims wouldn't be nearly as high as the cost of paying fees to all those doctors.

Insurance companies being what they are about money, the next step was obvious. And so today, if you're young enough (under forty-five, as a rule) and wish to buy not too much insurance ($30,000 is the usual limit), you can forgo a medical exam when you apply, which makes getting life insurance a good deal more convenient.

Don't think for a moment that the company is really being reckless. The underwriters do reserve the right to ask your own doctor for a statement, and if your record makes the Selection Department uneasy, to insist that you take the full medical exam.

Eventually, whether you buy non-medical insurance or take an exam, and whether the policy is for $5,000 or $500,-000, the information-gathering machinery finishes its work and switches off. The results find their way from the various sources of information, through channels, to the home-office underwriter's desk, perhaps the most beleaguered outpost of the company's enormous paper empire. The average underwriter carries a daily load of between ten and thirty cases. On any given day an underwriter for one of the top two hundred companies will exercise his power of final decision on at least five of those cases. His method of assessing your risk potential is a kind of contest between you and a set of averages, with the underwriter acting as umpire. This contest is called the Numerical Rating Method.

Under the Numerical Rating Method, the underwriter must analyze your case under eight different headings: family history, race, occupation, habitat, medical history, personal habits, physical condition, and build (height and weight in correlation). In each area he has at his fingertips the norms derived from studies of the thousands (or millions) of people insurance companies have already insured. The underwriter grades you on the basis of how you fit the *normal* characteristics under each of the eight headings. A grade of 100 means that in a given area you closely match the thousands of others who according to industry experience attain normal life expectancy. If you score *higher* than 100, you're a poorer-than-normal risk in this area because you match up with people whose chances of dying prematurely are greater than average. If you score *lower* than 100, the hazards of the area in question touch you less severely than they do most people. Thus, you're a better-than normal risk. Your better-than-average ratings offset your poorer-than-average ratings in a complicated system of debits and credits, so it's your total score that counts.

The rulebook makes much better sense if we actually play the game, so let's return to that set of assumptions we made in Chapter 1. You are once again a man aged thirty-five, married, with two children. You've climbed part way up the executive ladder at a major corporation to a job which pays $12,000–$15,000 a year. You live, mostly, within that income. You already own some life insurance. In addition, the insurance company knows that you own your suburban home, that you drink in moderation but smoke a little too much, that your parents are still in fair health, that you yourself have had only one serious ailment, and that you're five feet ten inches and weigh a hundred seventy pounds.

As things stand, your case won't even reach a senior underwriter. A clerk will screen your file, stamp Approved Standard on it, and shove it along to the policy-issue section— unless the amount of insurance you applied for is grotesquely more than you can afford to carry. In all eight areas your numerical rating is 100 or less (better than average). You're almost too good to be true.

Suppose you have a stomach ulcer, painful and burdensome, but not disabling. According to the statistics, ulcers do have measurable effects on mortality (as, say, appendicitis doesn't), but those effects are relatively slight. So you can get life insurance, but you may have to pay an extra charge of $5 per $1,000 of insurance each year, at least temporarily. To your annoyance, your agent will tell you that you're "rated up" (in the industry's peculiar phrase) for insurance.

To make real sense out of medical underwriting, we must consider a range of examples. At one end of the scale there are all these ailments which have no effect (as far as the actuaries now know) on how long you live: the childhood diseases, minor bone fractures, and so on. At the other extreme lurk the destructive diseases: coronaries, cancer, multiple sclerosis, and the rest. The mortality hazard depends not only on the kind of ailment but on the severity or mildness of the attack, the quality of the treatment, and your age and physical condition.

At one time the only medical reasons for extra insurance

charges were gout and *not* having had smallpox. Today the underwriter must be able to assess the possible mortality consequences of everything from chlorosis (green sickness, an adolescent anemia that post-Victorian girls rarely incur) to parrot fever. Fortunately, medical progress and the revolution in gathering and processing data make the underwriter a very capable diagnostician.

If all the hazards affecting human life were medical, his job might be easier. But other problems besides those of illness and disease threaten us, and some of these other hazards don't lend themselves to precise diagnosis and rating.

Suppose we restore you to good health but take away your good financial standing. A few years ago you ran up a pile of debts, and finally, struggling to repay your obligations, you made a deal with some of your creditors at fifty cents on the dollar. A little later you applied to your bank for a loan and were advised not to press the application. The local department store still lets you charge but has you pegged as a "slow payer, $75 top allowance." In short, though you've been scrupulous in recent years, your credit is suspect.

You might ask indignantly why such a situation would affect your insurability. Surely the underwriter doesn't think you're going to rig up some kind of plot to defraud the company? Besides, all that trouble happened several years ago, and you've learned your lesson and reformed. Does the company really care about something that's nobody's business in any case?

The underwriter isn't concerned about anything as dramatic as fraud. His company's investigators (and the police) are well able to handle such an eventuality. But your financial history does tell the underwriter something about your attitude toward new obligations. With the industry's lapse ratios (or percentage of dropped policies) what they are, no underwriter wants to "buy a lapse" for his company. His concern isn't for the money you loose when you drop a policy, but for the loss to the company.

Because life insurance companies are the most lenient of financial institutions, only a very small percentage of applicants—about one half of one per cent—are rejected because of bad credit. But that comes to a total of 125,000 people.

Now let's make a final change in your background. In addition to being a solidly successful middle-class citizen, you possess one additional characteristic.

You are a Negro.

As an executive, a substantial earner, and an excellent health risk, you're a decided cut above the American average. In order to gain your status in our present society, you are very likely an exceptionally able individual as well. Being a Negro does *not* mean that you are barred from obtaining life insurance at standard rates in one of the major companies. But this fact in turn does *not* mean that you're exempt from discrimination.

In the cold-blooded terms of the underwriting trade, your race is a strike against you. Negro mortality rates are markedly "adverse" in comparison with those of whites, for reasons which should be grimly obvious to every citizen. As a Negro, you'll be debited Numerical Rating points because of your color. In your particular case these points will be off-set by the points you've presumably built up by being an executive, financially secure, etc. Because your personal, medical, and other histories are favorable, you'll probably overcome your basic handicap. But if you were poorer, sicker, or more sinful, you wouldn't.

What is true for you as a Negro is also true for Filipinos, Chinese-Americans, American Indians, Mexicans, and Puerto Ricans. The industry's patterns of discrimination can't help mirroring American society's discrimination. This is another case where statistics reflect our cultural habits back at us with an evil wink.

This final unhappy example of how you are measured against the statistical norms highlights one side of the truth about insurance underwriting. The process of selection is mechanized and made routine—so much so that even the final step, the act of decision, seems to be automatic. Some companies are experimenting with computerization of the entire underwriting procedure. Programmers translate your personal statistics into computer language and feed them into a machine. A master program instructs this computer to compare your statistics with the norms, referring if necessary to the information storehouse within its electronic memory. Because the process of comparison is so often tantamount to actual selection, some experts think that 90 per cent of all life insurance can actually be ratified by machine.

But no mere machine can really cope with, say, a $500,000 life insurance application, because such big policies, or "jumbo risks," invariably defy all the normal rules and standards. The man who needs and can afford $500,000 worth of insurance is no ordinary applicant. He is undoubtedly a financial success who needs no education in the virtues of life insurance. Precisely because he is successful, this applicant knows the score—a fact which always makes an underwriter nervous. "I always wonder," one senior underwriter said, "what he knows about himself that I don't know."

The flaw in the crystal might be anything: a lawsuit, a jealous mistress, a peculiar Dun & Bradstreet report. Here let's suppose there's a tinge of sugar in his urine specimen. From the rest of his medical history, this applicant is unlikely to be an incipient diabetic. But that flicker of change in the laboratory litmus paper is enough to set the information machine spinning all over again. The salesman will be the luckless messenger who must let the customer know that things aren't quite right—that the company wants the customer to take a Glucose Tolerance Test.

The applicant won't be pleased to learn that he must fast for twelve to eighteen hours, then spend an entire morning in the medical laboratory drinking a nauseating glucose concoction while his blood-sugar level is measured. But the home office won't settle for anything less, so the unhappy agent goes off to convince the recalcitrant customer. After days of backing and filling, the customer goes through with the test.

Typically, the results are an underwriter's nightmare: smack on the borderline between normality and excess. Also typical is an applicant who's fifty years old and fifteen pounds overweight. What's more, the applicant is probably known to like a drink, or two, or three. He's by no means a "steady free user" (the underwriter's picturesque phrase for a near-alcoholic), but still . . .

If everything else—and that means *everything*—looks good, the applicant *may* get standard insurance. If so, the sweat disappears from the salesman's brow and he makes his reservations for the Million Dollar Round Table convention at the Greenbrier. The applicant may permit himself the luxury of an inward smile of triumph as he reaches for his checkbook.

To cover a jumbo risk, an insurance company takes a special precaution known as "reinsurance." To a life insurance company, this practice is what "laying off" a bet is to a bookmaker. Whenever such odds-takers assume a risk larger than they want to afford, they share that risk (by prearrangement) with other odds-takers. In return, the originator gives up a piece of the action—or, in respectable insurance terms, a proportionate share of the premium. Even the largest companies reinsure their jumbo risks, allowing themselves only a certain percentage of the total for their own "retention." If all goes well, reinsurance cases are profitable for the reinsurers who get enough such business to spread their risk, because no commissions or other sales expenses are involved.

Reinsurance is too technical a subject to cover in depth here. But it is important to remember that such comradely sharing of risk implies the sharing of information as well. This means that one insurance company can quite easily find out what other companies know about you.

In fact, the industry maintains a central Medical Information Bureau in Boston, where for decades records have been kept of every single applicant's insurance history. Subscriber companies have free access to these records. Until recently (1964), any insurance company was able to learn whether a competitor had ever rated you up or turned you down. It took a court decision (suggesting that such back-scratching might be an antitrust violation) to end this particular exchange of information. But the fact still remains that whatever one insurance company knows about you another can find out.

The jumbo risk is only one of the problems that can make the underwriter's life difficult. A good way to get to the heart of underwriting is to glance at a few more problem categories and to note what puts the underwriter on the defensive as far as approving candidates is concerned. Then we'll have a better understanding of the industry's appraisal-and-selection philosophy.

For example, a problem that may be at the opposite end of the scale in size from the jumbo risk is the one raised when grown children apply for insurance on the life of a parent. "Now why after all these years," asks one underwriter, "should Junior suddenly want a policy on dear old Daddy?" To the underwriter, this question is purely rhetorical. He sees the situation as a classic example of anti-selection. By exposing the company to a poor insurance risk, Junior is trying to wangle a pay-off despite the dictates of the mortality table (see Chapter 2). As far as the underwriter is concerned, it's too late for dear old Daddy to climb on the bandwagon. "Funny, but I somehow feel that Junior's working against me," this underwriter added, and the statistics bear him out.

Related to the problem of anti-selection is that of "moral hazard." For the underwriter to judge insurability in terms of moral habits, he must subordinate his own feelings of right and wrong to what the statistics tell him. For instance, homosexuality, whatever stigma it carries, is not grounds for refusing or rating up life insurance. There's no evidence whatever that the homosexual's longevity norm is lower than average. On the contrary, notes one underwriter, "we may conclude that homosexuals are . . . law-abiding, hardworking, and above average in education, intelligence, and rating."

On the other hand, the question of "insurable interest" is critical in estimating possible moral hazard. Whether or not someone has the legal and moral right to be your beneficiary depends on his having a valid relationship to you. That's why an underwriter will automatically look dubious if you name a friend as beneficiary. Does your friend really stand to lose so much because of your death that he has a legitimate reason to become your beneficiary?

Such intangible areas as anti-selection and moral hazard stand in sharp contrast to problem areas where statistics comfortably confirm the underwriter in his decision-making.

Thus, if you're a steeplejack or a sandhog, a high-steel worker or a telephone lineman, you might logically expect to pay extra for insurance. Such occupations present obvious hazards, and underwriters place so-called "occupational ratings" (from $2 to $15 extra a year per $1,000 of insurance) on workers in these jobs. If you quit climbing around on steel girders and turn to some other line of work, the rating will be removed. But don't take up bartending or any other work connected with the retail sale of liquor. Though you personally may be a teetotaler, your new job carries an occupational rating like the old; liquor, according to the underwriter, is an automatic hazard. Liquor stores are often robbed, and to the Selection Department, bars are scenes of violence and headquarters for illegal activity.

One of the highest-rated (i.e., most expensive) occupations in terms of hazard is that of Air Force jet pilot. Even in peacetime, companies charge anywhere from $5 to $20 extra per $1,000 of insurance, depending on age and flight experience. "That's not a fair assessment of the extra mortality cost, just our way of discouraging applicants," according to one rating official. "A *fair* charge would be a hundred dollars per thousand. We might break even that way."

At the other extreme, professionals are "preferred risks," and some companies even offer special policies to doctors, lawyers, accountants, and architects. Because by nature underwriters enjoy making fine distinctions, selection experts will tell you that among physicians, a radiologist is a better risk than a surgeon (there's less danger of infection in the x-ray lab than in the operating room). Likewise, a staff accountant is a more favorable risk than an outside auditor because he's less exposed to the hazards of travel and his job isn't as likely to tempt him into embezzlement or fraud.

However, such distinctions are only academic as far as life

insurance is concerned. At this upper end of the preferability scale, your major problem is keeping insurance salesmen from breaking down your door.

The insurance salesman himself is a standard, but not a preferred, occupational risk. Like other outside salesmen, the insurance man faces slightly higher "travel risk" exposure than does the man at a desk. The fact that home-office underwriters generally feel sorry for agents doesn't mean a thing as far as getting insurance is concerned. Occasionally, perhaps, an agent who's on the borderline between insurability and uninsurability gets a break out of professional courtesy. But equally often the Selection Department bears down harder on the agent than on the outsider because, as one unsympathetic underwriter put it, "those guys know all the tricks about what to hide."

While we're discussing occupational hazards it may be illuminating to observe that professional criminals are frequently able to obtain insurance; especially if their crimes are such non-violent ones as gambling or jewel thievery. The expert crook with "good protection" can often buy what a man with a single criminal conviction cannot, since the pro has the means of concealing his criminal activity and background. Moreover, the truly professional outlaw isn't very often that most fascinating of underwriting freaks, the "target risk."

As the phrase implies, a target risk is the individual whose life is by definition a perpetual hazard or for whom even a tiny incident can be a catastrophe. The movie star, the professional athlete, the big-name entertainer—such figures are target risks. The combination of high but unpredictable earning ability (which makes these people so valuable to their families and associates), vocational uncertainty, and uniqueness all add up to the abnormal, in exactly the sense

98 ·

which underwriters dread. Because target risks are so precious to so many people, publicly and privately, someone is always calculating the economic worth of a celebrity's physical life.

For example, think of the crowd of people whose livelihood depends on the talent and performing ability of a popular singer. Costume and stage designers, make-up men, accompanists, arrangers, song writers—these are only a few of the specialists who have staked their own careers on the success of one performer. Add to that list the manager, the agent, the publicity and promotion men, the recording companies, the motion picture and television interests, and you have a clearer picture of the small-scale but weighty universe the star entertainer carries on his shoulders. No wonder, since show business is Big Business, the big-name star is so often heavily insured.

Most of the policies we read about are short-term propositions taken out by, say, a producer for the duration of a film contract. Many such policies only insure against accidental death. By limiting the insurance, the producer keeps his cost low—and gets what he's really looking for: publicity.

That publicity, as far as the underwriters are concerned, is deplorable, because the million-dollar policy focuses public attention on the aleatory (or gambling) nature of life insurance. That life insurance is a betting proposition somehow takes on more significance when it's a prominent personality whose life is insured. Nothing makes company management more uncomfortable than to have the public reminded that insurance is other than a staid, conservative financial arrangement. But business is business, so insurance underwriters throw away the rulebook, and working by intuition and a considerable amount of experience, they underwrite the target risk.

Deviations from the norm—jumbo risks, morals hazards, and occupational and target risks—only point out how powerfully the norms do govern underwriting. Indeed, if there weren't millions of us who, by leading safe, normal lives, counterbalanced the relatively few "risky" risks, the industry couldn't afford either its steeplejacks or its million-dollar-policy owners.

The industry has every right to protect itself and its present policyholders against an equivalent to a run on a bank: an avalanche of *poor* risks. As a matter of fact, during 1964 approximately 750,000 people were refused insurance, while another 1,200,000 were rated up, mostly for medical or occupational reasons. (Outright turndowns ran about 3 per cent of total applications, while rated-up policies totaled about 5.5 per cent.) It would seem that the life insurance industry is doing an excellent job of preserving the safety of what the companies have previously harvested.

But aside from rejection or rating up of poor risks, life insurance underwriting also involves a different kind of selectivity: discrimination among various classes of plausible risk. In an industry as big as life insurance, such discrimination is present in many forms and in many subtle gradations. For example, one agency manager (in New York City) could actually say, in the presence of his company's home-office underwriting officials, "Don't sell any niggers life insurance. We don't want them, we won't write them, and any salesman who messes around with them will have his contract terminated." You can be certain that the salesmen took this manager at his word.

At the company's home office, a top sales executive tried to put the matter in a different light by saying, "We are glad to accept whatever Negro business comes our way. But we don't go out looking for Negroes to insure."

This executive then "explained" that existing Negro business, while not as safe for the company as white business, caused the company's actuaries no serious concern. (He didn't say why.) "But," he added, "we have no intention of trying to increase our share of non-white business, because to increase your share of *any* market is expensive. And if we're going to spend the money, we'd rather spend it on more profitable policy owners."

Within any company the range of attitudes will run from crude bigotry to a more sophisticated hypocrisy. Implicit in such attitudes is the idea that a Negro applicant can get decent treatment and good insurance somewhere *else* among the industry's 1,700 companies: but not here. In short, a Negro is allowed to buy life insurance if—and only if—he keeps trying until he finds a company or agent who won't either reject him or else steal him blind.

We're not referring only to the South, where local white insurance companies either bar Negroes or—in a fashion characteristic of much Southern business—*specialize* in Negro risks and hire Negro agents to peddle insurance to them. Nor are we referring only to Texas and the Southwest, where Mexican-Americans as well as Negroes face the identical pattern of rejection and exploitation, the two going hand in hand. We are talking about an uneven and blotchy disease that afflicts the entire American life insurance industry like a pox. For some companies welcome Negro business in general, some companies welcome *some* Negroes, and some welcome none at all.

In cities with important Polish, Ukrainian, Italian, or Hungarian minorities, an insurance company may operate agencies just to exploit such markets—but at the same time discourage its other agencies from submitting Polacks, hunkies, wops, or whatever the degrading term happens to be. Do these companies, with their national reputations as guardians of financial rectitude, discriminate? Not to hear their public relations executives talk. But if you still wonder whether or not such discrimination is based purely on estimation of risk, just listen to their underwriters in the shirt-sleeves atmosphere of the Selection Department. Not always, but enough of the time to be sickening, their supposed "adverse mortality" is a flimsy excuse for exercising simple prejudice.

Besides racial bias, there is discrimination based on age. The industry's underwriters have faithfully adhered to the averages in influencing their companies to sell to younger buyers instead of older people. Though surveys show that many Americans in their fifties and sixties are both interested in and able to obtain life insurance, the underwriters' preference for "new, young lives" has diverted attention away from these older prospects.

And although underwriters have known for decades that women outlive men, only within recent years have a few companies begun to offer lower insurance rates to women. Yet in one American family out of three, the wife is a full-time breadwinner, and presumably a key to her family's financial security. At the behest of the experts, she too is neglected by the salesmen.

It's wrong to lay all such discrimination at the Selection Department's door. But the underwriter's bias in favor of what one specialist called "the bright-eyed young executive with .1 house, 1.0 wife, 2.3 kids, 20/20 vision, 120/90 blood pressure, and a future life expectancy of 40 years" does drive the salesman still further along the road he wants to travel anyway.

Underwriting practices are all the more curious—to say the least—in the light of another principle. If you stood on a street corner and (without any selection whatever) insured the first 1,000 passers-by, the results in terms of mortality would be almost as good as those yielded by the elaborate selection methods we've just been analyzing. The sheer randomness of such apparently devil-may-care underwriting *is* your safeguard against buying too many bad risks for the company.

As a matter of fact, this we-insure-all-comers approach is the basis of group life insurance, which many of us carry where we work; and group underwriting has for fifty years been tested and proved successful. For all their exactitude, individual underwriting procedures are awkward, expensive, and inequitable by comparison. The industry well knows that underwriting can be done safely for a fraction of its present cost. Just as some Agency System executives know that the industry's distribution methods are outmoded, so do many actuaries realize that underwriting is antiquated and narrow. But so far there has been very little pressure to change things—except that existing procedures are being mechanized.

Why?

The answer is that the underwriters, like everybody else in life insurance, are concerned with the preservation of the system as it stands. To tamper with the mechanics of selection, to make life insurance easier to get, is, so they say, another form of discrimination—against the millions of policy owners who got *their* life insurance the hard way. And such discrimination, we're meant to believe, might even jeopardize those immense reserves of money that the companies control. "If we do anything," one chief underwriter said, "we'll tighten up underwriting."

This means that although you are healthier, stronger, and longer-lived than your parents were, when it comes to buying insurance, you'll benefit only very slightly—if at all—from such blessings. The real beneficiaries of this improvement in public health are the companies themselves. For though you're a better risk, they'll charge you the same old rate your father paid—and take their time about returning, in the form of dividends, even a portion of the money they don't need. Here's where normal insurance conservatism shades off into something close to pure exploitation.

Let's make one final point. Obviously the most important feature of life insurance selection is that the more normal and average *you* are, the easier it is for you to get life insurance. The more normal and average *everybody* is, the happier the insurance underwriters are. This doesn't mean that a bohemian, for instance, can't ever buy insurance. But "normalcy" does have a special value.

In 1964 this institution sold nearly 21,000,000 individual life insurance policies, 10,000,000 of which required the special attention of the industry's underwriters (the balance being in amounts small enough to permit routine handling). When a local department store screens a few thousand charge-account applicants, the standards for granting credit are its own affair. But when the life insurance industry selects its customers, its standards cease to be of local or passing concern. They take on the impact of a social force. Given both the standards and the scope of present-day insurance selection, life insurance as an institution inevitably strengthens conformity, regularity, and safety. The logic of selection thus leads to a paradox: insurance without *any* risk to the insurance company.

"Our real problem . . . is what to do with all that money."

—*the Investment Specialist*

6 . How to Make
$7,000,000,000 a Year

"ALL THEY HAD was two pieces of paper. But because of that paper, we lent them eight million dollars. That was twenty years and a hundred and fifty million dollars ago. We were right then, and we're still right today—I only wish we had more of it." The speaker leaned back in his chair and brushed a speck of dust off the lapel of his beautifully tailored suit. At that moment he looked exactly like what he was, a financier who had backed his own judgment with hundreds of millions of dollars. And by means of such investments, this relaxed but formidable-looking gentleman had helped build not a single business, but entire industries.

At a desk in the antechamber outside the first man's comfortable office, a young fellow with the foulard tie and neat haircut of the Ivy Leaguer bent over a folder stuffed with papers. "Here's an interesting one," he said. "The client owns a string of bowling alleys out in Ohio and Kentucky. He wants to absorb a drive-in-movie chain and some restaurants. Says he can do what he wants with just a million. But I don't like those figures on the alleys. That business is overextended, so . . ." His hand reached out for the telephone.

The two men could have been father and son, managing between them one of our country's larger family fortunes. Despite the difference in age, each of them had the prosperous look and self-confident manner that comes from being used to money and money decisions. But neither of these men makes such decisions as we've just heard about for his own account.

On the contrary, the money they handle belongs to you.

As a life insurance buyer, you probably don't spend much time thinking about what happens to the money you pay the company. One reason you buy life insurance in the first place is that you're told experts should take care of money matters for you and solve your most serious financial problems. So once you own life insurance, you naturally assume that the financial affairs of your company and the industry are watched over with unceasing care; and indeed they are. But you still have the right to know just how the industry does stand guard over your money, for as it turns out, the decisions of the experts affect far more than the value of your policy. Without your being aware of the fact, the industry's investments have shaped and are still shaping the life you lead—as a consumer, a businessman, and a citizen.

This chapter deals with the investments made by life insurance companies, with the sophisticated and unexpectedly dramatic ways in which financial experts move an incredible $150,000,000 from the industry's coffers into the economy *every working day*. This is a bottomless subject. The American economy is so complex and variegated that it defies ready explanation, and life insurance investments lie at the heart of our economy. So perhaps the only way to start is by taking certain things for granted. For instance, you can assume that an industry which in 1964 invested a total of $34,000,000,000 is subject to special legal regulations in handling investment money. You can also assume that the practical realities of running a life insurance company have a restraining effect on the company's investment procedures. Anyone in the business of "guaranteeing money for future delivery" (as the insurance agent likes to say) must make certain that his investments are conservative.

Most people make the mistake of equating conservatism with a lack of enterprise; and for reasons that will become obvious, the experts don't make a point of correcting that mistake. But it's possible to be both conservative *and* venturesome—to play things safe and still come out far, far ahead.

One other thing we must take for granted in our economy is the presence of a market for money. We normally think of that market only in terms of Wall Street and the New York Stock Exchange, in images of ticker tape and the financial page. In reality, the money market is much broader and more embracing than the traffic in stocks and other securities. To analyze this market in detail would mean discussing the great commercial banks, investment houses, and other immense lending institutions—including life insurance companies. But this is no place for a treatise on lenders or on the machinery that keeps the funds flowing between them and their opposites, the borrowers. Here we can only point out that because this complicated machinery works, the money market is a real market: a meeting place for buyers and sellers of money, a constantly shifting scene of negotiation, successful dealing, and failure.

The size of this market for money only obscures the realities behind money-bargaining. Although everyone realizes that vast sums of money and complex deals are the rule, it is easy to forget the obvious. Institutions themselves, such as U.S. Steel and General Motors, don't mysteriously come alive to bargain for the money that sustains them. Men do this bargaining, and other men are the lenders; and still others grow rich by assisting such bargainers to come together. This makes the money market what it really is—a tangle of private strategies and public contests, partly a jungle and partly an exclusive club of insiders.

The money market has created its own particular breed of men. Well-dressed, well-educated, pleasant socially, these men usually come from the right schools and live on the right side of the tracks. We've all met, or at least know about, such men. They're mostly Republicans, but not necessarily political conservatives, and certainly not the kind who start noisy arguments about politics on the commuter train or over the luncheon table. Beneath their affability lies a shrewdness and sophistication about money which most of us totally lack. Whether these men work for law firms, banks, investment houses, or life insurance companies makes no real difference, for actually they are all in the same business, that of buying and selling money.

Such men are the reason why in the investment arena a life insurance company behaves differently from the way we've seen it behave so far. Quickness and skill enable insurance companies to be as subtle, calculating, and ruthless as any other moneylender. To measure that skill, simply consider that the job of a life insurance investment specialist involves a paradox.

Every time you pay a premium, most of that money (expenses aside) must be farmed out to earn interest, or else presumably the company will find itself in trouble; i.e., unable to meet its guarantees. So while the company's salesmen scramble furiously to sell more insurance and bring in more money, the investment experts also scramble—

decorously, but just as hard—to get rid of that money by selling it at interest to the buyers in the money market. But unlike selling life insurance, this investment race is no game for clumsy amateurs. To direct your company's share of that $150,000,000-a-day money flow into *good* investments, especially while your competitors are likewise combing the market, is anything but easy.

This explains why an insurance company's investment specialists are a select, even an elite, group within the company hierarchy, completely unconcerned about the routines of sales, underwriting, service, or other operations. ("They even eat lunch by themselves," one executive from outside his company's Investment Department noted.) The exacting techniques of investment analysis—culling information from balance sheets, understanding profit-and-loss statements, checking credit, making field surveys—require much more elaborate training than most life insurance executives ever have or need. It makes no difference whether the specialist belongs to the securities or to the mortgage branch of the Investment Department, although most companies do split their investment activities into these separate divisions. And to specialize further within either area takes research talent and more than a little imagination. Finally, to be given responsibility in dealing directly with the company's money-market contacts and clients, the investment specialist must be a member of the club. That is, he must speak the same language as the bankers, lawyers, real estate entrepreneurs, and financiers.

Aside from being on good business terms with such key money-market personalities, the insurance-company specialist should also be able to golf or go hunting with these other club members. Sharing their pleasures as well as their business habits is important because while you may compete against them today, you want to do business with them tomorrow. The ideal recruit for the Investment Department is a rare combination of brains and social connections, equally at home in a Wall Street board room or in a duck-blind on the St. Lawrence. That a life insurance company pays its investment men more money and treats them with more respect than other employees should come as no surprise.

For both legal and practical reasons, life insurance companies diversify their investments, spreading them over many different industries and sectors of the economy. The given company further avoids hazard by dispersing its investments geographically and over long periods of time in terms of maturity. Such diversity makes the company's Investment Department the nerve center of a complicated network; it is a combined intelligence service and source of new investments. Each specialist has personal contacts in the money market, and they keep him supplied with information about his own investment area (or areas, since many specialists oversee activity in more than one field). The department's access to investment information and to would-be borrowers provides a steady stream of raw data. We'll focus on several specific investment areas: bonds, real estate, and corporate finance. To see how the process works, let's look first at a relatively quiet sector of the money market, municipal bonds.

Because their safety is backed by a community's power to raise revenue, "municipals" are a natural investment for an institution that must keep one eye on the safety of its money. An insurance company's municipal-bond specialist sees dozens of such bond offerings each week, and his immediate problem is simply to decide which municipals to buy.

If the bonds in question are the city bonds of Chicago,

110·

the expert doesn't have to wonder whether the community's credit is solidly based. Chicago's bonds are invariably sold through investment banking syndicates of great respectability, so the insurance-company specialist can be sure that the facts and figures in the bond proposal (or prospectus) are straight. If the interest yield, maturity dates, and other features of the loan all accord with his needs and his budget, then the specialist merely calls a favored contact at one of the participating investment banks and tells him, "Put me down for a million dollars of Chicago." The transaction is just that easy.

But suppose, to take a purely hypothetical example, that the town of Dare, Georgia, wants to raise $500,000 to build an airport. Though the amount of the loan is trifling to an insurance company, the specialist's problem is considerably more complicated. His old crony Charlie, "a damn good municipals man downtown," has written him a note recommending these obscure bonds. But where *is* Dare, Georgia, anyway? And why should Dare's city fathers want an airport? Charlie's prospectus gives some of the answers: Dare is a county seat; location, northeastern Georgia; population 8,700. But why does such a town anticipate air traffic? The prospectus only mentions "anticipated industrial development in the immediate vicinity," but something is stirring in the back of the bond specialist's mind.

He calls another friend, the vice-president of an Atlanta bank. This local contact reminds him that a large corporation has just announced plans to build a factory right on the outskirts of Dare, Georgia. In fact, the friend goes on, another man in the bank was born in Dare, and he says that his home town is in the throes of a boomlet. Other plants are springing up in a new industrial park, the local farm economy is stable and thriving, there are few racial problems, and so on.

Reassured that Dare is growing and prospering and that an airport will eventually stimulate that growth, the bond expert also knows that a couple of the crusty bankers on the company's Finance Committee are eager to make loans to small communities along the Southern coast. Then, too, that large corporation whose plant is rising in Dare may soon be floating a loan of its own, and these municipal bonds might be a way of getting in on the ground floor . . . so the bond man calls Charlie and takes on half, or more, of this little-noticed bond issue. Charlie thanks him gravely, knowing full well that each has done the other a favor. Indeed, this minuscule investment might pay off in far more important business later on.

In today's municipals market, subtler tactics bow to the fact of competition. Brokerage firms, which can resell municipal bonds directly to the public because the interest income on municipals is tax-exempt, bid sharply against insurance companies and other investing institutions for the privilege of lending money to communities. Since the investor that makes the loan at the lowest interest rate wins, bond-issuing municipalities now have real bargaining power on the money market.

But before their special tax status made municipals widely attractive, life insurance companies were the most powerful purchasers of these bonds. During the 1940's one of the biggest companies had a municipals specialist who could boast, "I can make or break any town in this country." And a major company's withdrawal from the bidding can still turn city finance officials pale.

Now, with competition strong, good contacts are more important than ever. "Charlie downtown" can do a lot of favors for a friend in a life insurance company. "Take that West Virginia Turnpike issue in 1957," one specialist said. "Charlie and I had lunch on that one. He didn't open his mouth except to mention that the highway engineers they were using happened to be the same firm that had made the toll-revenue forecasts on a certain turnpike in 1956. So I didn't buy West Virginia, and they haven't covered their interest on the loan yet."

To call such subtle interchanges of information "collusive" is downright insulting. There's certainly nothing illegal about buying Charlie lunch and afterward talking investment shop. That's simply the way the money market works —even for a life insurance company.

In the insurance-investment game, the bond market (which also includes state bonds, utility, railroad, industrial, and federal bonds) is considered a relaxed, cozy corner of the money-market club. Even though during 1964 life insurance companies did buy $1,000,000,000 worth of bonds *a month*, the pace of this trading is relatively easy. But that's not true of the money market in general. In those areas where the bargaining is wide open, life insurance men are known as real horse traders.

For example, take the case of a well-known real estate developer, a specialist in shopping centers. Like many of this breed, the gentleman operates on a hair-thin margin. As he tells the story, "It cost me every dime I had just to assemble the land package" for one now famous shopping center. "I even borrowed from an uncle of mine, a real thief. But I got the whole thing together and I went out and got tenants. What leases!"

(The essence of shopping-center finance is to use the long-term leases or lease commitments made by solid tenants—

department stores, chain shops, and the like—as collateral for short-term loans to finance construction.)

But this developer ran into trouble. "My general contractor was a crook. His subs [subcontractors] were animals. Animals. The buildings aren't finished by deadline, and my tenants are ready to kill me. They sue, and I'm dead. It's 'Go collect from the bonding company.' " At the very thought, he shifted uneasily in his chair.

"So one day what do you think happens? A couple of guys, a regular team, comes in my office. They're from a big life insurance company, they tell me, and they been watching this center like a hawk. Not only that, but they've got a proposition. They'll buy me out and then lease the property back to me to operate for them. Am I interested?

"So I tell them sure, figuring what the hell do they know about shopping centers? And right then and there the one guy whips open his briefcase and comes up with an offer that, so help me God, was one cent away from being grand larceny. They may not know about shopping centers, but those guys sure know about money. They'd been to my bank, they'd been to my tenants, they'd been everywhere. And by the time *they* spread out their deal, even my uncle looks like a philanthropist.

"Naturally I laugh and tell them, 'Gentlemen, forget it.' But a week later they're back with a new proposition, and to tell you the truth, after taxes this one doesn't look so bad. Meanwhile, all this time I'm getting calls from my tenants' lawyers. If I don't get this thing finished, they invoke non-completion clauses, and I'm a stiff.

"So to make a long story short, I sell out to the life insurance company for never mind what. They put the center up, and I'm operating it for them. They got the property, and what am I? A landlord, an agent, that's what."

114·

You may think of the life insurance industry's real estate investments in the pious terms of company literature or industry-association brochures. "Through . . . mortgages," goes one such account, "life companies provided housing for millions of people, financed thousands of farms and business properties, and are helping to underwrite the revitalization of the urban centers as well as suburban areas of scores of cities." But the truth is that such statements tell only a small fraction of the story. Today life insurance investment in real estate is a coldly commercial proposition, one built on a tiny measure of risk, a very high margin of safety, and the hope of enormous rewards.

Right after World War II the insurance industry did pour hundreds of millions of dollars into the financing of private (one-to-four family) residences. But especially during the last decade a momentous shift in investment strategy has changed that picture. The reason is that in home financing, life insurance companies found themselves fighting a losing battle against the local banks and savings-and-loan companies. These local money merchants have a double advantage. They know their communities and their real estate better than an insurance company can, and they don't have to pay a commission to a broker, mortgage correspondent, or other middleman. In order to compete successfully with loan rates offered by a life insurance company, a local bank can reduce its mortgage rate from, say 5.5 per cent to an even 5. To you, as an individual borrower, that half per cent reduction may be worth only a few dollars a month. But to the insurance company, that rate-shaving means a ten per cent loss in total income from mortgages, a loss of perhaps $15,000,000 or $20,000,000 a year.

Faced with this unappetizing prospect, life insurance companies turned to other ways of making a dollar in real estate.

So while they're still carrying billions of dollars' worth of residential mortgages (most of them from a day when rates were higher), many big insurance companies have entirely shifted to investment in commercial real estate or in multi-family apartment dwellings.

A special way of advancing funds for such projects, known as "forward commitment," has been the real estate specialist's chief tool in shifting his company into larger-scale and more lucrative realty deals. Simply by promising to lend money to a borrower *after* his building is constructed, the company can help the borrower find enough credit to do the actual construction, thus creating a future investment without any risk whatever. Under forward commitments, life insurance companies today are involving themselves heavily in what their literature may call "the revitalization of urban centers," but which are really the big, speculative office buildings springing up on expensive urban sites all over the country. Such multibillion-dollar projects greatly stimulate the building trades, providing jobs for construction workers and money for contractors. But whether the end results "revitalize" anything is a moot question. In the words of one city planning expert, "Financing those glass boxes certainly lines the pockets of the big real estate speculators, and the banks and insurance companies get an excellent return. But good Lord, they're ruining the cities!" And she may have a point.

In bonds and real estate, life insurance companies don't generally handle money like the benevolent institutions they say they are, but what about the third investment area, corporate loans? Here we are back in the world of high finance, where what takes place is cloaked in the esoteric language of the money men. But if we can manage to do what corporate lawyers always say they're doing, and "pierce

116·

the corporate veil," what we find may make us very thoughtful. So let's look in on a cliché-ridden little drama.

The scene is the board room of a big corporation, one of those vast, mahogany-paneled chambers so dear to the hearts of important businessmen. The characters are all executives, including as the star the president of the corporation. His supporting cast consists of a couple of life insurance investment men, and discreetly silent in the background, there are one or two representatives of the go-between, the investment bank that has brought the insurance men to its client, the big corporation.

"This is going to mean a great deal to all of us," the president says. "I hope your people are as happy with it as we are."

"The Finance Committee is especially delighted with those repayment arrangements," one of the insurance loan experts answers. "But we'll naturally want a man on your board. And for the first couple of years I think we'd better have monthly rather than quarterly financial reports. You'd have no objection to that?"

"None whatever. We'd welcome somebody like you on our board."

"Well, we'll have to see about that. Maybe it better be one of our officers."

As the conversation dwindles, the president suddenly relaxes and invites everybody down to the officers' private dining room for a good lunch. Obviously, these men have just consummated an important deal. But what kind of deal?

This ritual was the formal closing of a $20,000,000 loan, the borrower being the corporation, and the lender, the life insurance company. Surely it seems miles removed from the textbook assumptions that life insurance companies invest subject to legal regulation and report their investments faithfully to state insurance departments, so that their investment procedures are entirely open and straightforward.

You have just seen why most corporate investments made by life insurance companies are not known to the public. This loan transaction was concluded strictly between the principals, in what the money market appropriately calls a "private placement."

By the end of 1964 total corporate indebtedness to the life insurance industry had reached a fantastic $35,300,000,000. Of this total (according to the authoritative *Life Insurance Fact Book*), "an estimated $30 billion . . . was acquired through direct negotiations with the borrowers, rather than through the purchase of bonds . . . [Such] transactions are loans made directly to corporations, secured by notes . . ."

That is, *six sevenths of this immense corporate indebtedness is money that has changed hands privately, in deals kept secret from outsiders.* In such deals, life insurance companies take your money into partnership with great commercial and investment banks for the loans that nourish American business. Through these private transactions, the life insurance industry quietly exerts immense power in the money market, and thus on the entire free enterprise system. And no one, not even the federal government, can fully know all the details of these transactions.

This direct-borrowing method dates back to the middle 1930's, when businessmen first experimented with raising money in ways that side-stepped regulation by the still young Securities and Exchange Commission. Thanks to the enthusiastic co-operation of the life insurance industry, private placement has—especially since the war—become the preferred norm for corporate borrowing. Today such private deals originate wherever business strategy dictates the need to use somebody else's money: in the headquarters of businesses whose stock is owned by hundreds of thousands of people and in the offices of firms tightly controlled by a few insiders. A given private placement may involve no more than a trifling (for an insurance company) $250,000 for a new factory. Or it might mean an incredibly complicated financing program for a corporation the size of a General Motors (whose own great postwar expansion got its start from just such a private loan—of $100,000,000). But the point is that any business can go to a life insurance company and borrow quietly what the investment specialists determine it can afford. Moreover, if the deal looks good to the specialist, even a multimillion-dollar loan can be arranged within thirty days. "It takes longer to buy a ten-thousand-dollar policy than it does to borrow five hundred thousand dollars," one investment man wisecracked.

This special form of corporate finance enables life insurance companies—despite their so-called conservatism—to become deeply involved in industries with spectacular growth, and even to take part in what most of us would shy away from as speculative ventures. As a tool of investment strategy, private placement permits individual companies to back new or unusual businesses, thus probing the edges of the economy and opening up new areas for investment years ahead of the rest of the industry.

Twenty years ago most life-insurance-company Finance Committee members trembled at the thought of Texas oil. "Guys wearing ten-gallon hats and cowboy boots were always showing up in New York and talking about millions of dollars," one investment officer recalls, "but most of us wouldn't listen." Even the Wall Street venture capitalists backed away from these oilmen and from the few investment banking firms (White Weld & Company was one of the first) which did see merit amid all the apparent risk.

The Texans had an answer to the question of risk: pour so much money into exploration that by the law of averages major oil discoveries will have to be forthcoming. Then develop these finds on the largest possible scale and sell the oil to distributors—meanwhile, avoiding like the plague what one oilman called "all them there gasoline stations." Texas money was available for exploration, but large-scale development was too expensive for even Texans to handle.

Fascinated by this investment opportunity, one New York insurance company (which had already lent some mortgage money to pipe-line builders and therefore already knew something about the oil business) did send an investment officer down to Texas to look further into oil deals. Through a complicated set of financial arrangements, this company entered privately into one such deal as early as 1945. Today this company's investment in "petroleum and related industries" stands at $180,000,000. Despite some low-yield oil-company bonds the company bought in 1946 ("unfortunate," the oil specialist calls them), the current return on that investment is a juicy 5.6 per cent. By 1967 that return will rise to nearly 7 per cent. Indeed, on one or two of these deals the total yield may run as high as 9 per cent. Not bad for a "conservative" lender.

Moreover, grateful developers keep bringing in other deals to this company's now experienced oil-investment experts. Such contacts have given this company almost total dominion over the petroleum-financing field. "Of course, we do get a lot of competition from the banks," the oil specialist pointed out. "But other life insurance companies— they have a hard time getting in unless we *invite* them in."

The foregoing is a classic case of the life insurance investment man's dream of a little-known business development that needs big money to make it work. "We're in the wholesale money business," observed another investment officer. "We'd *always* rather sell a lot of money at once than a little bit here and a little bit there. Of course, now we're big enough to go wholesale. Some of our little competitors, well, they're better off staying in bonds."

Another interesting case in point comes from the automobile rental business. "Now it's a billion-dollar industry," one investment banker said of this business, "but fifteen years ago, it was full of racketeers." More important, most auto-rental firms were struggling, undercapitalized corporate infants. After all, people *bought* cars, and in the years right after the war, the real money was seemingly in the selling (and financing) of automobiles, not in their rental. Only a few insiders understood then the real potential in car rental. "It's simple," said one of them. "If you can buy the cars cheap enough from the manufacturer, you can run the hell out of them for a year and sell them used at retail for almost as much as you paid wholesale. So your rental income's in the clear, and you've got depreciation allowances besides." This terse summary should be enough to show that once a rental firm reaches a certain size, it turns the corner and begins to make big money. "In this business you need enough dough to buy just one big fleet, and that's it."

Once again the insurance industry as a whole shied away from the new and unfamiliar. But one company's investment analyst was able to convince his superiors that because of tax advantages and sheer convenience, renting rather than owning automobiles would grow greatly in popularity. In making his presentation to the Finance Committee, he shrewdly concentrated on *commercial* rental: "We sell these deals to the committee harder than an insurance agent pushes his policies. And I figured that the picture of a big corporation renting whole armadas of automobiles would look a lot more solid than the idea of individual rental."

As a result of his report (a masterpiece of research and skilled forecasting), the investment man's own company, together with one or two others, offered private loans to one of the smallest but best-managed auto-rental concerns. "Over the past ten years we've let them have about eighteen million dollars. And we've lent to other rental-company borrowers as well," the specialist commented. "Now they come to us for financing and tell the banks to go jump."

Everything we've seen so far about life insurance investment in general and corporate lending in particular tells us that your money and mine goes not only into nice, safe bonds and mortgages but also into newer and livelier forms of investment. The image of a life insurance company as a fat-cat moneylender interested in nothing but safety is projected purely for propaganda purposes. Actually, so hard do companies look for juicy investment opportunities that the industry sometimes does strange and wonderful things with the dollars of its 120,000,000 policy owners. To see what sometimes happens, let's look in on another meeting—one a good deal less formal than that held in the board room of a few pages back.

We're now in the special conference room kept available by one of those super *de luxe* businessmen's motels that you find out near the airport of any good-sized city. Two of the room's three occupants, in shirt sleeves, are busily sliding papers into their briefcases. The third, a sharply dressed man in his middle forties, is plainly thinking aloud.

"Our biggest problem all along has been the summer slump. But with this help, we can really put on a big push for the vacation market. I hear that in Dayton a couple of companies are actually selling more to the resort trade than they do around Easter. You guys are really giving us room to swing . . ."

The first two men are life-insurance-company investment specialists on a visit from the home office. But who and *what* is this speaker? From his conversation he sounds like a local retailer, and in a way that's exactly what he is. But this gentleman's stores don't feature ladies' and girls' finery or children's toys. His retail business sells only one product: money.

You may be surprised to discover that one of the newest and biggest customers the life insurance industry has found in recent years is small-loan-and-finance companies, whose second-floor walkup offices are the outposts of a multibillion-dollar credit empire. Most of us do know, or should know, how these outfits work. Their specialty is quick cash, and they prefer really needy borrowers, people whose extravagance has already put them into debt. In return for their few-questions-asked-just-your-signature loan service, such firms charge really horrific rates of interest, 12 to 20 per cent or more. And woe betide the debtor who gets behind on his monthly payments!

In today's prosperous, credit-oriented economy, this small-loan business is growing so fast that its biggest headache is keeping an adequate supply of money on hand. Nothing frustrates a loan-company treasurer more than the thought of his company's running out of money while people are lined up to borrow at 20 per cent. But in peak seasons, just before Christmas, for example, that possibility becomes very real. And a really prosperous loan company *never* brings in enough customer repayments to take care of the needs of new borrowers. Therefore, rather than risk being caught short of cash, the loan outfit will itself borrow from a bigger moneylender, usually on a series of 90- or 180-day repayment notes (but sometimes on a longer-term basis). And what

123·

lender has more money to spare than the life insurance industry? In 1964 it put $680,000,000 into these credit outfits. Needless to add, the insurance companies most active in this lending area don't advertise that they are in effect the bankers of the small-loan credit sharks. Company officials understand only too well why you might find it odd for your life insurance company (which preaches thrift and sells mostly policies that indeed *force* you to be thrifty) to finance a business that reaps its own profits from your extravagance.

This last example tells us exactly why private placements are such a great boon, not only to corporate borrowers but to life insurance lenders as well. There are certain other businesses (tobacco and liquor companies, for example) that also offer safe, lucrative investments but with which the industry would rather not be publicly associated. There may also be individual firms whose trade practices are unsavory but whose investment potential is big, where life insurance investment men prefer to slip in by the back door. Then, too, there are the obvious embarrassments. "You couldn't expect people to understand," said one investment official rather sheepishly, "why we'd want to lend their money to a casket company."

Whether or not we approve of their desire for privacy, there's no question about the skill and finesse with which insurance companies move money around. Because the investment men are so impressively expert, you'll never have to lie awake nights wondering whether the company that insures you is financially strong and solvent. If anything, the investment wizards are too ingenious. "We've got money lying around all over the place," one investment man said. And then he added wearily, "If you really want to know the truth, our problem is figuring out what the hell to *do* with all that money."

The following may highlight the investment man's dilemma. "Memo to All Agency Managers: You will be pleased to learn that the company's auditors have recently found $3,000,000 worth of bonds which have evidently been missing since 1955. Investment Department officials had not noticed that these securities had been dropped from the company's inventory. Our quarterly audit this season turned up the bonds in the company's basement vault. This humorous occurrence might make an effective testimony to our financial strength when mentioned in your agency meeting."

Sure enough, the company in question had somehow lost its $3,000,000, which but for a chance discovery might have been written off the company's books (or at least not turned up for years). But when you've got as many billions of assets, misplacing a few million doesn't really worry anyone.

This "humorous" incident points to a much more serious matter. Many close students of life-insurance-industry economics feel that most companies are far, far richer than they need to be. After intense technical analysis of the industry's financial condition, a Harvard Business School professor, James E. Walter, draws a three-fold conclusion: (1) company reserves are worth *at least* 10 to 15 per cent *more* than even the most stringent state laws require; (2) surplus funds (those kept on hand in addition to legal reserves) are in turn worth an additional 10 to 15 per cent of the reserves themselves (substantially in excess of requirements); and (3) investment income, year by year, is running *at least 30 per cent higher* than is necessary to maintain company financial coffers at their present over-full levels.

Thus, as a matter of routine, insurance-company financial experts are keeping a cushion of roughly 30 per cent more than they need legally and actuarially to insure the lives of their present policy owners and to expand at current speeds.

This same cushion, moreover, is built into the investment process (and also into the premium-rate structure) to make sure that the future picture will remain unaltered. If Professor Walter and his scholarly colleagues are correct, the implications are tremendous. Taking the industry's total assets as in excess of $150,000,000,000, our life insurance companies have evidently accumulated a treasure of $45,-000,000,000 that will *never* be needed to pay claims and will *never* be returned to us or to our beneficiaries. As things stand, that $45,000,000,000 can do only one thing: grow.

The mere presence of such incredible wealth is disturbing enough. But certain other facts make the situation even stranger and more alarming.

Within its Investment Department a major life insurance company typically houses no more than forty or fifty securities and real estate specialists. Only some of these men are actually empowered to make financial commitments on the company's behalf, and their decisions are in turn subject to the approval of an even smaller Finance Committee. (This select policymaking body is drawn partly from the Board of Trustees and partly from the highest ranks of management, including the president.)

The Finance Committee's members are almost always themselves key men in the outside financial community. This means that the company's connections with the money fraternity are guaranteed to be superb. But the truly frightening fact is that taking senior specialists and active Finance Committee members into account, no more than three or four men actually direct the investment affairs of one of these multibillion-dollar investment giants. It has been estimated that 1,000 men control among themselves all the investments of the two hundred top companies.

This must be the greatest concentration of financial power

in private hands that society has ever seen. The nature of the funds under their control is such that without impairing in the slightest any company's ability to fulfill its commitments, the caretakers could easily become corporate plunderers on a truly gigantic scale. Despite elaborate and accurate systems of internal financial control, only the personal honor and sense of stewardship of the industry's investment overseers stands between an immense fortune and the temptation of private greed.

But the concentration of public money in private hands —as dangerous as this may be—is only one side of the coin. Trustworthy men, not greedy money barons, have built up the industry's treasury, presumably on our behalf and for our safety, not for private gain. And some insurance-company experts defend the industry's vast surpluses and acquisitive philosophy by stating that in case of war, depression, or other national catastrophe, the country never need doubt the industry's strength.

But other experts—an increasing number of them from within the industry—find such reasoning out of date and much too defensive. These authorities minimize the possibility of management dishonesty but insist that such an overflowing treasury encourages careless, inefficient management and frightful waste. According to what we ourselves are discovering about the life insurance industry, these authorities seem to be only too correct. Furthermore, you may feel—with justice—that your company has no right to make you pay extra for "security" that you don't want and that not even the strictest laws require. "That's not insurance, that's a forced saving," you may rightly understand.

Like so many others, however, you may decide that when it comes to buying life insurance, you're helpless: you have no choice but to accept the *status quo*. In a later chapter we'll see how helpless you are and whether there aren't at least partial solutions to your dilemma. But you can be certain that the great money craftsmen who handle the industry's investments are going to go on working at their trade. Their operations will be screened from your view. Their prestige and power will go unchecked.

You aren't supposed to know that the real estate experts are straining for investment success to the tune of 8 or 9 per cent a year. You are definitely not supposed to find out that life insurance companies are bankrolling the nation's small-loan operators—and thus helping to sell your savings back to you at 20 per cent a year. And even though you don't profit by the results, you are *never* supposed to question this industry's right to drive unceasingly for ever greater gain. You can certainly conclude that the experts who handle your money have forgotten whose money it is and what that money is supposed to be for.

"Most of these fellows could play golf four or five times
a week and it wouldn't matter."
—*former insurance-company President*

7 . *Power Failure—at the Top*

DURING THE 1880's AND 1890's, when the American life insurance industry had already grown great, Richard McCurdy
was the president of The Mutual Life Insurance Company
of New York. Like so many of this industry's early rulers,
McCurdy was a fabulous promoter, a money baron in the
grand style. He was also something of an autocrat. At precisely four o'clock each afternoon, McCurdy would rise from
his desk and stride out of his office. At the door a flunky
would hand him his hat and stick. His personal elevator had
to be ready. Outside the Mutual Life home office, a smart
carriage and pair stood waiting to carry the great man to the
ferry that took him across the Hudson on his homeward
route. And if for some reason McCurdy's arrival at the pier
was delayed, the ferryboat waited.

Today the president of Mutual of New York is a gentleman named Roger Hull, a soft-spoken man whose subordinates call him by his first name. Mr. Hull would no more
keep the Weehawken ferry (in his case, the commuter train
to Darien) waiting than he would shove his way to the head

of the ticket line. As befits a modern insurance executive who happens to have been bred a Southerner, Mr. Hull prides himself on being the soul of courtesy.

And yet, Roger Hull shares with Richard McCurdy more than high office in the same company. As the president of a major mutual-insurance enterprise, Mr. Hull is no more accountable to the owners of his company—let alone to the public at large—than was Mr. McCurdy himself back in this industry's gilded days. Autocratic or not, and the insurance industry still has more than its share of autocrats, the life insurance chieftains and the senior executives who surround them are the lineal descendants of the royalists, the imperialists, of American business.

Today's life insurance executives don't go around shouting, "The public be damned!" the way railroad magnate William Vanderbilt did about the turn of the century. After all, this *is* the era of public relations, when, as someone has remarked, "in one generation, Du Pont has gone from being 'Merchants of Death' to giving people 'Better Things for Better Living Through Chemistry.' "

But the men who run our life insurance companies today are still the absolute masters of their individual empires and of the entire industry. They run the life insurance business the way they want to, and nobody can sue for a reckoning.

To see how top management in this industry can retain such total control, let's first look briefly at what goes on outside the realm of insurance. For instance, General Motors is the largest private industrial enterprise in the world, with over $10,000,000,000 worth of assets, with sales that surpass $15,000,000,000 a year, and with yearly profits in excess of $1,000,000,000. Like all giant corporations, General Motors is managed by a team of company-minded specialists who strain to keep G.M. a supremely powerful business entity.

General Motors also likes to brag about the number of people who own its stock. Over 1,000,000 Americans hold shares in this enormous, and enormously profitable, business. With that many of us dividing the ownership, no wonder G.M.'s dividend checks take the form of computer punch cards. Whatever you call this huge, diffuse shareholding system— "people's capitalism," "economic democracy," etc.—it's obvious that the management can't possibly explain to each stockholder the whys and wherefores of the company's behavior. But you can bet that if General Motors has a bad, or even a slightly less than sensational, year, management will hear rumblings—or worse—from the stockholders. Even the most minor error can arouse a chorus of complaint. "If the paint job on a few Cadillacs isn't what it should be," one G.M. regional executive commented, "we'll get a thousand letters, all starting off: 'Dear Sirs: As a stockholder of General Motors, I don't think you're doing a very good job . . .' "

Because their money is so obviously at stake, shareholders don't take lightly the ventures, or misadventures, of those who manage American business. Almost overnight the owners of a publicly held corporation can become first an articulate pressure group and then a hanging jury for a maladroit management. In many corporate situations a small but sophisticated minority will be watching and waiting to move in. "Nothing keeps management honest," said a corporate public relations specialist, "like knowing that a bunch of strangers might take over ownership control."

Furthermore, in most businesses an even more vocal and sophisticated pressure group is always lying in ambush for management: the customers. Long before the stockholders begin baying for management blood, the people who use the company's products will have started to spread the word that Old XYZ & Company isn't making widgets the way it used to. Because they, too, have money at stake, the buyers sit in perpetual judgment on the way the seller runs his business.

But what happens when a company is owned not by a few thousand or even 1,000,000 people, but by 5,000,000 or 10,000,000—or as in the case of the Metropolitan Life Insurance Company, by 45,000,000, especially when none of those owners, no matter how much money he's got, can ever possess more than a minuscule share of this vast enterprise? How can the policyholders, who are the legal owners of a mutual life insurance company, possibly form a cohesive ownership group to bring pressure, or even to exert indirect influence, on the company's management?

To take one graphic example, every mutual-company policy owner is legally entitled to attend the annual meeting. Can you imagine what would happen if, say, a fraction of one per cent of Metropolitan Life policyholders decided that this was the year to attend? Yankee Stadium wouldn't hold that meeting. But such a thing could never happen. Indeed, so few policy owners are aware there *is* an annual meeting that Metropolitan Life can announce the location of its meeting as the board room at the home office.

So much for the influence of insurance-company *ownership* on management.

And as far as the influence of insurance *customers* is concerned, forget it. In life insurance, of course, there is no well-defined, articulate body of purchasers. Because we buy insurance in private, we have no way of knowing who else owns a policy. Only the company can know who its customers are; the customers can't know each other. Therefore, no individual, no group of buyers, and certainly no National Association for the Protection of Policy Owners exists to ride herd on the men who manage life insurance companies.

So the question remains: To whom is this management

responsible? Well, we do know that life insurance, like banking, transportation, communications, and utilities is a "regulated industry," whose practices are scrutinized closely by special state commissions. Presumably the industry's top management anwers to these regulatory bodies, if to no one else.

But not a single insurance commission is able (or, in some cases, willing) to do an adequate job of policing this industry.

New York State has perhaps the most stringent insurance laws of any state in the country. Yet according to an employee of the New York State Insurance Department, who for obvious reasons declined to be identified, "As much chicanery, double-dealing, and swindling goes on in New York as anywhere else." At great length this department employee explained that his office (the New York City branch) was understaffed, its workers underpaid, that it was impossible to enforce the complex regulations of the state insurance code, and that as in so many similar situations "politics" dictated an expedient compromise.

"When it comes to financial matters, these companies more than obey the letter of the law. We send in auditors and find everything in apple-pie order." The prime concern is that companies be unassailably solvent. "As long as they've got enough money to pay all their claims, and as long as they stick to the prescribed investments, *we don't really worry about what they do.*" (Italics added.)

In short, the New York State Insurance Department interferes as little as possible with actual company operation. "Sometimes we advise a company in a friendly way that it better discontinue certain practices before there's trouble. But it's pretty friendly, and they [the company executives] know where to draw the line."

A perfect case in point is the department's Complaint Bureau, where you can report any difficulty you have with an insurance agent or broker. "What we try to do," said one complaint investigator, "is make an example of one or two agents a month. We catch some guy who's clearly defrauding the public, we hold a hearing, we take his license away, and maybe even get him indicted on a criminal charge. Then we publicize the case in the life insurance trade press.

"We hope that keeps the rest of the agents from really going overboard. And we do follow up on other complaints. But we can't really keep tabs on everything that's going on. There's forty of us in the Complaint Bureau and about twenty-five thousand insurance agents in New York City alone. So we pretty much have to trust the companies to police themselves."

As long as the financial regulations are observed (and what big life insurance company has solvency problems?), the industry has little trouble with state regulatory commissions, in New York or anywhere else. Because they have no legal liability for the misbehavior of their agents, the companies can and do disavow any act by an agent that gets him in trouble with the customer or the law. And since life insurance companies are a major source of state tax revenue, top state officials are very careful about treading on the industry's toes.

So if you suppose that life-insurance-company top management goes in fear of legal regulations or regulatory bodies, you had better reconsider. On the contrary, life insurance officials fraternize closely with their friends in the insurance departments. "The legal departments of the big companies are full of ex-department counsels. Former heads of state insurance commissions are in demand to sit on the boards of insurance companies. You couldn't exactly say there's a fight going on."

This all adds up to one conclusion. The individuals who manage our biggest industry operate entirely according to their own lights. Life insurance companies are so powerful that they help write the laws under which they're regulated. As a result, the laws don't regulate them very well. Neither ownership nor customer groups influence management behavior, so the industry is largely exempt from the checks and balances that govern our business community. The consequences of this immunity are disturbing, to say the least. In a society that prides itself on being able to control and contain powerful vested interests, the life insurance industry answers to no one, no one at all.

As a result of such freedom from restraint, three things have happened within the life insurance industry. First, top management has formed itself into a good old-fashioned oligarchy, the kind that used to be called a citadel of special privilege. Second, the administration of life insurance companies has become notably incompetent—even for an era when every citizen spends much of his time struggling with wayward bureaucracies. Third, the industry's products and attitudes both reflect the indifference the life insurance businessman feels toward the public he purports to serve.

Starting with a sketch of top management at work and then broadening our focus to take in technology, communications, and political habits, we'll examine evidence of this severe malfunctioning.

As you may suspect by now, part of the price we pay to have life insurance is a management system so complex and so bureaucratized that even specialists in company organization are bewildered. But even the biggest company must have a top—a place, as Harry Truman once wryly noted, "where the buck stops." In a life insurance company, the place is occupied by a committee. At the nominal head of this group of senior executives stands a single official to whom most companies give the title of president.

You can imagine how these top executives have gained their eminence. Step by slow step, they have crept up through the ranks of one or another specialized management hierarchy: sales, service, underwriting, law, or investment. By the time they reach the top, the members of this group are almost always middle-aged men within ten years of retirement. Practically without exception, these senior officials have spent their entire lifetime being loyal to their industry, often serving only one company. Collectively their job is to determine company policy and to govern the company as it ploughs ahead, year by year, into the future. From their predecessors, men now elevated to the Board of Trustees, retired, or dead, these executives have inherited a going concern, frequently massive in size and scope.

All they really have to do is keep going.

In one sense, nothing could be easier than to keep a life insurance company going. Like any other big enterprise, an insurance company is self-operating, and the bigger and older the company, the more automatic are the processes of growth and renewal that keep it alive. A distinguished executive, once the president of a huge insurance company, brought to life this aspect of insurance-company management in a pungent comment about his former colleagues. "Most of those fellows could play golf three or four days a week, and it wouldn't make any difference at all."

The image is a good one. The leisurely nature of the life insurance business, not to mention the shelter afforded by all those layers of management beneath the top, is perfect insulation from urgent problems or emergencies. For generations the life insurance business has been a comfortable executive haven, in which high officials have been able to lead pleasant and sociable business lives. Not every insurance-company president plays his golf at Burning Tree or spends his winters at Hobe Sound. But in general, this industry does take good care of its top brass. The private dining rooms, the company hotel suites, and the clubs and resorts of the top business elite are familiar territory—if not hereditary fiefdoms—to insurance executives.

These men make pretty good money, too. The going salary for the president of a big life insurance company now ranges from $80,000 to $200,000 a year. The president's senior subordinates generally take home earnings in the $50,000 bracket, and any good-sized life insurance company carries on its payroll dozens of officials who make more than $25,000. While any business must obviously pay its executives well, it's hard in this context to forget that "average successful salesman," who works a lot harder than these officials and makes only $4,000 a year.

Because the industry's biggest companies are self-renewing and secure, a top manager's job is largely one of encouraging the troops. Since in recent years Americans have bought lots of life insurance, high company officials are convinced as never before that everything's coming up roses for their industry. In fact, some senior executives unhesitatingly ascribe the industry's record-breaking sales to the personal co-operation of God Almighty.

No other modern industry attaches so much importance to God's personal participation as a kind of high-level consultant to top management. At conventions, for example, not even the most tasteless meal can be consumed without invoking the Deity in terms like the following verbatim transcript: "Almighty God, bless this food we are about to receive. Bless this fellowship of devoted, dedicated men. Bless this company, which exists only to do Thy will on earth. And especially bless our great president [president's name] and give him strength to lead us ever onward. In Christ's name we ask this. Amen."

Granted, the life insurance business has always been evangelistic. For the most part, the nineteenth-century fathers of the industry were stoutly Victorian and Christian businessmen who enlisted salesmen under the life insurance banner as soldiers of the Lord. Given the service overtones present in a life insurance career, it's not surprising that many devout men choose to make their livings from life insurance.

But most other businessmen have long since realized that in our pluralistic society many religious people are deeply affronted by this yoking together of God and Mammon. The life insurance industry alone seems not to have outgrown the strident religiosity of men like Bruce Barton, whose proclamation ran, "Jesus Christ was the greatest Salesman the world has ever known." Significantly, one major company's president proudly identifies himself with the "Crusade for Christ" of revivalist Billy Graham, the minister whose preaching draws heavily on the secular rhetoric of salesmanship, and whose faith, neatly packaged and consumer-oriented, communicates itself to the public via all the techniques of mass persuasion.

"The Old Man may think God is doing all the work around here," one of this president's subordinates commented drily, "but it's a damn good thing we've got a smart Investment Department." To which we might add that from what we've seen about this industry's practices, the only Christian thing about life insurance is its militance.

Even the non-religious among top insurance executives exude faith—in themselves and their own good works. Since top management's basic task is to sell and resell the virtues of life insurance to a captive audience of salesmen and sales managers, such displays of faith have taken on all the aspects of ritual. Witness, for example, the life-insurance-company convention. Every year most insurance companies assemble their field personnel for several days of hotel living, recreation, and continuous exhortation by a management team with the president at its head. According to the author of *So . . . You're Going to Run a Convention,* Jack R. Morris of the Republic National Life, "the total amount of money that insurance companies spend on conventions is so astronomical nobody would believe it." (According to a conservative estimate, $1,000,000,000 of the policy owners' money is spent on conventions each year.)

This money is laid out to preach the same old lesson to the already-converted: life insurance is the greatest concept society has ever produced; all life insurance men have a great mission; the company had a great year last year and must have an even greater one this year. At convention time the inevitable gaps between actual and hoped-for performance are papered over with self-congratulation. The only important thing is that this is a great company, that business has never been better (you should see the speeches they made during the Depression), and that insurance men are indeed lucky to be alive. "We've got to do an even better job of keeping things going the way they've been going," was one rah-rah convention speaker's mystifying message. And this vice-president's "dynamic spirit" and "heartening statement of faith" won him special praise at the final banquet.

Spreading the message of faith takes up about 60 per cent of a life-insurance-company president's time. Otherwise, he's either performing the routine duties of a top-level administrator—attending board meetings, preparing reports, reviewing the decisions of his subordinates—or enjoying the special privileges of his office. By virtue of their high position, these

men are almost all prominent members of the Money Establishment. This means that they have their private investments to look after, their pet charities to pursue, their special
projects or hobbies to follow up. "You've got plenty of time
for outside activity in this job," the former company president quoted above pointed out. "Your Board [of Directors]
encourages you to be active in community affairs, charities,
and the rest. I used to think that *my* Board was happiest
when I wasn't in the office, trying to run things."

All the way down the line, life insurance executives are
similarly requested to take part in "community affairs."
Only the most innocuous projects, however, are really encouraged. It's no coincidence that the most popular extra-
curricular activity among top insurance officials (according
to a survey) is the Boy Scouts. Church work is a close second.
Local politics, of the uncontroversial variety common to the
suburbs where these executives live, is a remote third choice.

Life at the top in the life insurance industry is undemand-
ing and relaxed, a million miles removed from the rigors of
the agency manager's existence, let alone the terrors that
beset the agent. Not long ago the president of one of the
biggest companies decided, doubtless because he himself
had once been an agent, that all home-office executives who
hadn't come up through the sales ranks should "spend some
time as salesmen in the field." For at least one young executive, the experience was an icy bath. After six weeks of selling he quit. "I just couldn't go through with it," he said.
"Peddling this stuff to the public was the worst job I've ever
had."

To the man on the home-office ladder, a field assignment
can be exile to Siberia. To be offered a "temporary field
promotion" to agency manager is the life insurance equivalent of being told that "the Army no longer has confidence

in your leadership." Most recipients of this offer resign immediately.

On the other hand, to the "line executive" in the field, a home-office appointment means security, comfort, and a good living. "It's a hell of a lot easier shuffling papers than convincing salesmen to make one more call," was the way one home-office executive summed up his new job. So just as agency management is the special province of the con man, the hustling recruiter, the driving sales manager, so home-office management—especially in the Sales Department—is the barony of the supervisor who can't supervise, the executive whose superiors find him safe and whose subordinates laugh at him, and the vice-president whose most successful selling job was done on the executives who promoted him.

In short, life companies are successful businesses run by men who'd have trouble making a living anywhere else. Only because of the 500,000 agents at the bottom of the heap can insurance-company top management perpetuate itself in this easy corporate life. And only because the men at the top have no masters can they so exploit the men at the bottom. No wonder an outstanding management consultant calls the insurance industry, despite its record-breaking sales, "the worst-managed Big Business in America."

Indeed, throughout this book we've been documenting his opinion. The American Agency System, which a modern-minded management would abandon as soon as possible, is only the worst example of such inadequate leadership. And for all its horrors, the Agency System has seemingly been successful. For glimpses of a more obvious kind of management failure, we need only look at the effect of technological change on life insurance.

Almost every one of the processes that go on inside the

home office involves dozens of operations. These must be handled somehow, if not by people, then by machines. Thus, if one day you decide to change the beneficiary on your policy, you merely call your agent, who comes around with forms to sign. But these forms must travel through channels: first, from agent to agency; thence, to the home office; then, within the home office to exactly the right place. In this case, it's the Central Service Office, Customer Service Department, Beneficiary Unit, Policy Change Subunit.

There a clerk completes the necessary steps to record your change of mind on the company books, a procedure that will in turn mean changing duplicate records in half a dozen places. Finally, the company must notify the agent so he can let you know that your beneficiary has in fact been legally changed. All told, as many as ten different people must take time to attend to your minor problem. Multiply your own transaction ten thousandfold and you can see why life insurance companies need hundreds upon hundreds of employees. You can also see why automation (a term that covers everything from electric letter openers and pencil sharpeners to the most advanced solid-state computers) exerts a mystical spell over senior life insurance executives. Except for the postwar technological revolution in data-processing, the industry would have strangled in its own web of facts, records, and statistics.

Like banking and other public-service businesses, life insurance companies have invested billions of dollars in data-processing equipment. They have hired programmers, mathematicians, and other specialists to serve their new machines. They faithfully update these electronic "factories" whenever new developments threaten to make them obsolete. So this industry does seem to endorse, and even to worship, the most striking of our recent technological advances. But in reality life insurance officials feel they must make these huge outlays of policy-owner money just to keep abreast of their present workload. For instance, when told that his company was planning to install the newest, fastest, and most expensive computer system on the market, one director of customer service beamed happily, "Now maybe we'll be able to catch up on our paper work, for the first time in thirty years."

The "forward look" in life insurance technology, then, is basically defensive. Like a landlord who must keep on buying costly new maintenance equipment to keep his aging buildings in repair, the industry is pouring money into new technology merely to shore up sagging sales and service organizations. Life insurance officials are running faster and faster, not to modernize and thus revolutionize the service side of the business, but to preserve the *status quo*.

As a result, where in 1945 you could get your beneficiary officially changed in five working days, it now takes eight working days to get the same thing done. You can go six or eight *weeks* before the company notifies you about some policy details, and you may *never* find out what became of the expert who sold you your life insurance. Because growth without change is this industry's only ideal, the policy owner must wait, and never mind that he's an owner of the company.

If the Bell Telephone Company felt the same way about running its complicated business, the operator would still be asking to get your "number, please?" instead of your dialing almost anybody in the country within twenty-five seconds. Or if your bank decided to run its operation in the leisurely way life insurance companies do, you'd get a checking-account statement once a year instead of once a month. But then, why should life insurance companies give you better service? Who is going to make them?

Take another aspect of the industry's standards of management, what we can call "business communication." Most of us don't have to be reminded how strongly American business relies on advertising and public relations—not merely to sell, but also to inform and to create a favorable climate of opinion in which to do business. Although we may wince at diagrams of the human stomach in action, and while the fruity baritones and false gusto of TV commercials are often offensive, most of us do in fact pay plenty of attention to what business is telling us.

Such is the power of the word and the image that if an ad for an ugly car is written in sophisticated language, we're eager to believe that the car itself is sophisticated as well as of good quality. Because of that reaction, we've bought a great many Volkswagens. And because Kodak has spent a fortune to build a trustworthy reputation, we take Kodak's word for it when their ads tell us we can get great pictures by pointing *their* camera and pushing *their* button.

As effective as it is, advertising is only part of what American business does in the field of communication. For example, think of the IBM and Johnson's Wax pavilions at the New York World's Fair. Both companies are certainly profit-minded, commercially successful concerns. But they knew that in order to keep on making money, they had to *demonstrate* that they were decent and enlightened enterprises. They also knew that sometimes the best way to make the point is to say something that makes no reference either to the company or its products, but that entertains and educates the public.

In contrast, consider the following. Not long ago, a young public relations specialist wangled—by using pull and family connections—a chance to sell his talents to a large life insurance company. This young man had dreamed up an idea for getting athletes, adventurers, and other lively figures to endorse the company, and thus, in a modest way, brighten up the company's stodgy image. So he put together his presentation, went before the executive committee, and came away incredulous.

"They *liked* me," he said afterward. "I could feel that. But they simply didn't understand what I was talking about. 'Why should we use this, er, scheme of yours?' one nice old guy asked me. 'We don't need any *publicity*. We've already got one man doing that as it is.' " The young man shook his head. "They think public relations means killing the story about how the president's son got arrested for speeding on his way to Princeton."

The gentleman in charge of public relations later told the unsuccessful outsider that "hiring you is against company policy because we believe that every agent is our best public relations representative." When the young man answered that *he* thought the salesmen, instead of helping to solve the company's public relations problem, were *creating* that problem, the man from downstairs chided him for being so negative.

But that's nothing. Another company's vice-president in charge of advertising, sales promotion, *and* public relations stated, "We're thinking of changing ad agencies. Those guys have had our account for years without showing us any result at all. In fact, we may cut back our advertising budget substantially, from a million dollars to about four hundred thousand." When asked why, he answered, "It's a matter of cost. We think we could probably spend a lot of that money in other ways and see a much better return in terms of sales. We also think we could do without any fancy mass-media advertising (we're only in magazines anyway; we don't believe in TV—too expensive) and still not lose a nickel's worth of business."

As a result of attitudes like these, life insurance advertising is dreadful. There's no other way to describe how this industry presents itself to the public. True, the days are almost gone when you could count on a life insurance ad to strike the grim note of warning. "She May Well Wonder What the Future Will Bring," ran the headline on one early classic. The illustration showed a worried-looking young woman bending over the cradle of her sleeping child. Her husband, of course, had just died—without leaving her any life insurance.

Today most life companies will do anything rather than mention d——th. As a rough-hewn but effective way of making a survey, let's leaf through one issue of a major national weekly magazine and sample the life insurance advertising we find there. In this particular publication there are six life insurance ads, each on a full page (which, for a single insertion in black and white, costs about $10,000).

Of the six, three companies stress a single theme: our insurance is low in cost. Allstate says we can "Set up a $10,000 life insurance retirement nest egg—for $16 a month." State Mutual ties the economy angle to a health gimmick: "If you quit smoking one year ago, it'll cost you less to buy life insurance from us." And New England Life also stretches our dollars for us: "If you're earning over $10,000 a year, here are opportunities to make your income go farther."

You can buy that $16-a-month bargain from Allstate only if you're twenty-five; at thirty or forty it's not such a bargain. State Mutual is trying to persuade you that its rates are lower "for people who haven't smoked a cigarette in at least a year," but how will the company know? And New England Life's money-saving offer is the headline of an ad that asks you to buy *more* insurance (perhaps for your children) once your own "basic" insurance needs are solved.

146·

Two of the six companies, Bankers Life of Nebraska and (once again) Allstate, push sentiment. Bankers Life talks about "The Good Things Of Life" and offers us the drawing of a father proudly tying his young son's necktie. Judging by the prayer book and hymnal displayed in the sketch, the lad is off to church or Sunday school. By some strange coincidence, Allstate, too, shows us (this time in a photograph) a father tying *his* son's tie, above the glutinous caption: "Everybody's a little bit scared his first day of Sunday school."

Allstate is owned by Sears Roebuck, a company not noted for its indifference to profits. Allstate's agents do have a tremendous advantage over most other life insurance salesmen. The company offers cut-rate auto and household insurance to Sears Roebuck customers, as well as the general public, in part as a sales gimmick for Allstate life insurance. Bankers Life, on the other hand, is no such modern and up-to-date concern, just an old-fashioned, rich life insurance company using a pious ad.

The other two companies, Connecticut Mutual and Equitable Life, respectively threaten the businessman ("You'll be thankful for 'Blue Chip' coverage when a key man's chair is suddenly empty") and make pointless fun of the home buyer ("Only 359 payments to go and we own the house scot free").

As businessmen or advertising men, we might only sigh with regret for the wasted opportunities and dollars such ads represent. But as part of the *audience* for this advertising, we're more likely to be astonished, shocked, and bored. Instead of a message, each of these ads, and virtually all other life insurance advertising, gives us the spectacle of a billion-dollar American company sitting in the dark and mumbling to itself. Maybe, this inept advertising seems to say, maybe somebody will overhear and *do* something.

Faced with this lack of communication, we can't miss the implication that the men responsible for it simply don't give a damn. Not surprisingly, the favorite refuge of most insurance officials is the excuse that "we have thousands of salesmen making daily calls to remind people of what business we're in."

"Are you kidding?" one successful salesman asked scornfully. "Unless they insist, I never tell my customers *anything* about the company, not even the name." To ferret out by yourself the gaping crack in the industry's official logic, just ask yourself what you know about your own life insurance company or companies. (For instance, what company sold you your most recent policy?)

Life insurance leaders all act as if they believe in the conclusions of that advertising vice-president quoted a few pages back: "After all," he finally announced, "we don't need advertising. *The public already knows who we are and what we do.*" (Italics added.) When reminded that General Motors, Ford, Du Pont, Proctor & Gamble, RCA, and others are even better known, and that these companies nevertheless spend tens of millions of dollars each year on advertising, this gentleman had no reply.

His silence and his industry's mean exactly the same thing: profound ignorance of the techniques and the value of communication and profound mistrust of the communications process.

Such communicating as the industry does encourage is carefully processed, and all impurities are removed. If you ever have to ask an insurance company for some piece of general information, chances are you'll be referred to the industry-wide public relations organization, the Institute of

Life Insurance. There your inquiry will receive prompt attention and a careful—a very careful—reply. Broadly speaking, the institute is the industry's official herald and communications center. From its stylish New York headquarters (on Park Avenue), the institute runs elaborate advertising, educational, and public relations programs, all of which, naturally, present life insurance in the best possible light. These programs reveal as much about life insurance as the CIA tells us about American activity in the banana republics. Even so, however, most member companies feel that the institute simultaneously invades their precious privacy and yet absolves them from any need to create, let alone sustain, their own dialogues with the public.

From here we could go on to pin down the obvious. We could show how top management's beliefs about reaching (and reaching out to) that public are reflected all the way down the line. From high officialdom's personal unconcern and reluctance to speak freely, we can trace this entire industry's incompetence with words: its reliance on technical jargon, its pomposity, even the scrimshaw rhetoric of its latest canned sales pitches. And we could at last come to grips with why you get those letters addressed to "Dear policyholder:" that go on, "We deeply regret an error . . . Please be advised that . . . If you will complete and sign Form 591B (herewith enclosed) we will, pending receipt of satisfactory evidence, be pleased . . . Your remittance of $54.94 must, of course, accompany . . . Trusting that the aforesaid conveys the necessary information . . . Sincerely."

If we assume that life insurance communications, like those of other businesses, mirror the industry's feelings about itself, its products, and its public, then what? These dispirited ads, prepackaged public relations materials, and other lackluster efforts to break the silence point to some pretty dreary feelings. We are almost forced to conclude that this industry is uninterested in—and worse, contemptuous of—the public, unconfident about life insurance, and unwilling to do any more than thump its chest and grunt.

In business terms, reliance on direct selling and backwardness and ignorance about other ways of reaching the public are simply old-fashioned and out-of-date. Like sleeve garters, green eye shades, and steel pens, they evoke a management in love with tradition and fiercely resistant to change. One way to measure the effect of such conservatism on the life insurance business is to note that in 1950 life insurance companies controlled an unbelievable 50.7 per cent of the nation's savings. By by the end of 1964 life insurance's share of our national savings had dropped all the way down to 32 per cent. The industry's resistance to modernization has already cost it dearly, and industry officials would much rather pretend they don't know how fast that trend is moving against them. For the trend means that the enormous increase in sales, despite the ferocious exploitation of salesmen, hasn't kept pace with the even more astounding growth of our economy.

Another indicator that perturbs the gentlemen in the home offices is the steady decline in the premium they've been getting per $1,000 of insurance. It's not that insurance rates have been getting any cheaper. But people are buying less expensive insurance forms, for example, substituting the lower-cost term insurance for the more expensive permanent variety. So although the industry has sold more and more billions of dollars of insurance over the past fifteen years, the premium receipts per $1,000 have dropped from an average of about $22 to $12.38. In part, this deflates those dazzling sales figures and subdues the industry's grandiose claims to be more successful than ever. As always, the real victim is the agent, whose commissions are cut to the bone when the public buys term insurance.

These indicators or trends are nothing more than straws in the wind, disturbing but not terribly distressing to the men who run life insurance. Faced with statistics that measure what may well be a decline in the effectiveness of their salesmen, the industry's brass hats still don't feel the need to *do* anything. Instead, they're setting up industry-wide committees that never accomplish anything, holding seminars (usually at plush resorts) that end inconclusively, and going wide-eyed through other soothing rituals. Predictably, this management voodoo has produced no result, and every year the cracks in the system are a little larger. Even the management consultants, who today are finding the industry a fertile hunting ground for new, rich, and very willing clients, have thus far been of small help.

But such consultants are telling life insurance leadership that they do have plenty to worry about. Speaking before the 1962 meeting of the American Life Convention, Richard F. Neuschel, a senior partner of McKinsey & Company, Inc., told this select gathering of company presidents and their top-echelon subordinates just how badly in trouble they already were.

Neuschel began by citing "seven barriers to management vitality" in the life insurance industry, including in his list the "long lag between cause and effect," the "tendency toward rigid compartmentalization," and the "lack of executive mobility." In other words, things take forever to get done in this industry, there's no communication between the various arms of the business, and there's no vitalizing flow of fresh, outside management blood into the life insurance trade. Neuschel further commented:

the long-term decline in mortality rates has been, over the years, a factor of great significance. Few other industries have enjoyed the protection or the cushion of a force that can have the effect of making ordinary or even faulty performance look good.

Better medical care, a higher standard of living, and a prosperous economy—*not* any outstanding effort on the industry's part—are the real reasons for the industry's great postwar success.

Then Neuschel took apart the life insurance marketing operation (the Agency System) in terms of "the widespread need for strengthening the ability of . . . managers . . . *to manage a field sales force effectively.*" Following further brisk analysis of marketing shortcomings, he turned to the industry's internal troubles. About the performance of the vast life insurance bureaucracy, he had this to say: "Most managements would be shocked at the suggestion that reductions of twenty-five to thirty per cent or even more could be safely achieved in their administration costs." He further suggested that "the lure of the computer" had "produced a sort of electronic hypnosis among many managements . . ." Neuschel finished by indicating bluntly that "more attention needs to be given to . . . products and services that your customers *need*, instead of concentrating so heavily on making them want what you have to sell." In short, this industry must stop relying on salesmanship tempered with moral suasion and start delivering an honest public service.

We'll be meeting Mr. Neuschel again in the next chapter, when we take up the question of reform. For the moment let's stress that he was talking to an audience whose goals had—and still have—his complete sympathy. If anything, Neuschel's comments are more favorable in terms of the industry's image of reality than reality itself. Yet the shrillest

opponent of life insurance couldn't have put on record a
more damning indictment of this industry's management
record.

Nobody in life insurance spread the alarm or took up the
challenge; Neuschel's speech was given the absolute minimum of attention. In this industry why should anybody pay
attention even to friendly criticism? No outside critic of life
insurance really has power to make the industry live up to its
promise of service. Top management doesn't admit to its
ranks executives who want to change things, let alone improve them.

By now we shouldn't need to be reminded that the life
insurance industry is virtually its own narrow society within
our broader society. The industry has its own rules and its
own brand of orthodoxy, a brand so conservative that it
makes the conservatism of most American businessmen
seem like dangerous left-wing dissent. On the one hand, we
can see perfectly well why life insurance both attracts and
creates conservative management men. Despite all social
vicissitudes—wars, booms, slumps, and just plain "normalcy"
—life, death, and money remain the great human constants.
To deal in these primary staples of existence therefore requires a long focus and a conservative cast of mind. But on
the other hand, the conservatism of this industry's top
managers is also something else: the die-hardism of men
who have a great deal to lose if things do change.

In a typical magazine article for the trade, one president
of an important life insurance company stated that he (and
the industry) believes in "sound, economical, and honest
government" and in taking "an active, well-informed part in
. . . political and civic activities at home and on the national
level." Nothing could be more wholesome. True, this president's company *did* hire a former New York Assistant Super-

153 ·

intendent of Insurance to bolster its legal department and
plead the company's cause with his old friends in Albany.
But to read the president's phrases, you'd think all life insurance officials favored only such political theories as would
find favor in a seventh-grade civics class.

Despite such preachments, life insurance is one of America's most politically sophisticated businesses. The industry
spends millions of dollars a year on its Washington lobbies.
"We monitor and modify legislation, including that not
regarded as being in our best interests," according to one
expert lobbyist. What's more, from Augusta to Honolulu,
every statehouse has its own cadre of insurance lobbyists,
who hang around just to keep an eye on things at the local
level.

But at either level life insurance lobbies automatically
try to block, or at least water down, social legislation. For
example, the life insurance industry threw all its power and
influence into an anguished effort to defeat the original
Social Security Act of 1935. Washington resounded with the
screams of protest. Such lobbying reached another hysterical
peak in 1940, when the federal government put before Congress the National Service Life Insurance Act, the G.I. Insurance Bill. Life insurance officials went on record both
times, saying that Social Security and G.I. insurance would
"destroy" the American insurance industry. In local meetings across the country such organizations as the influential
National Association of Life Underwriters instructed tens of
thousands of members to write letters to their congressmen,
opposing these un-American bills. Fortunately for us and our
families, and for servicemen (who in wartime can't get private life insurance that covers them in battle zones), congressmen ignored such pressures.

It doesn't matter to the lobbyists that Social Security and

G.I. insurance have been of vast benefit both to the public and to the life insurance industry. As no amount of advertising or publicity could, these legislative programs focused public attention on life insurance and actually encouraged people to add larger private policies to what they got from the government. Many industry officials now say they knew all along that this would happen. Yet to this day, every time the government expands or extends our social insurance, life insurance lobbyists, like the geese who once guarded the Roman Capitol, begin to honk all over again. Only, unlike the real Capitoline geese, the guardians of our own Capitol Hill don't seem to know their friends from their enemies.

Furthermore, behind this industry's nonpartisan "good government" façade, top insurance officials carry on a great deal of *private* campaigning. Few industries gave Barry Goldwater's lost cause as much support as did the life insurance industry. If you read the minutes of such high-level industry organizations as the American Life Convention or just listen to the conversations of the top men at luncheons in the private dining rooms, you realize what the industry's real political alignment is. Not many businessmen speak so contemptuously about "Liberals," "Commies and Comsymps in government," and left-wing "bleeding hearts" (this last was an executive's characterization of Hubert Humphrey) without losing their colleagues' respect. Many senior life insurance officials are personally and unyieldingly committed to the Far Right. Though they're usually smart enough to keep their true sentiments hidden from policy owners, these executives don't hesitate to use their high posts as pulpits from which to preach their persuasions within the industry.

And yet, outside the industry insurance spokesmen remain completely silent on today's really critical issues.

With only one notable exception (to be discussed in the

next chapter), life insurance has had absolutely nothing to say on the subject of civil rights. In the selection of policy owners most companies are as discriminatory as the law permits. All companies practice the usual Big Business brands of anti-Semitism and anti-Negro discrimination in hiring management (as opposed to sales) employees. Naturally, though the industry has millions of minority-group, especially Negro, policy owners, the struggle for civil rights has struck insurance officials dumb.

The New York Times, covering the 1965 annual meeting of The Prudential Insurance Company, quoted the president, Orville E. Beal, as saying that "we do not discriminate" in the hiring of personnel. In the same interview, Beal conceded that his company's 20,000-man sales force included "no more than two or three hundred Negroes." Laying the blame on the shortage of "qualified Negroes," Beal insisted that the Prudential *was* doing something about it. "We've just hired a Negro personnel man." There have been stronger blows struck in the battle for equal rights.

Nor do the industry's leaders ever address the public directly on other key problems, even when such problems bear strongly on life insurance. Thus, we hear nothing about automation, the aging population, conservation of natural resources, or urban development, just to mention some of the important issues facing our society. Instead, the men who run our insurance companies confine themselves to safe, optimistic generalities: productivity seems to be rising; public health may be improving; and (thanks, of course, to the free enterprise system) America still offers glorious opportunities to one and all.

And so, we have a picture of this industry's top management. Sustained in office by methods that the rest of American business no longer believes in, left to themselves by owners, customers, and government, these men have made a private club out of our wealthiest industry. The members are apt to be men of considerable personal charm, who tell you with engaging frankness that it's hard to run a club these days; to find good servants is impossible, and the cost of keeping things up is just terrible, terrible. But this club has strict bylaws, and there is one rule which you mustn't break: do not criticize.

Because the industry is a society within a society, its members don't much care about what goes on outside. But now is the time when we have to care. After all, we're the ones who pay the dues.

For instance, most of us know that to drop a policy soon after taking it out will cost us money, not only the insurance protection we presumably need but most of the cash equity accumulated in the policy's reserves. Knowing this, why do we lapse *one new policy out of every four* within thirteen months of buying it? According to the industry's own surveys, the major reasons are (1) lack of money to pay the premium, (2) ignorance of the loss sustained, and (3) persuasion by a competitive agent.

The company's expenses are the same for lapsed policies as for those that stay on the books, and the cost of those lapses must be charged off somehow. To cover the company's loss, our premiums contain a built-in "lapse factor" of about 15 per cent of the annual premium. In short, we are penalized because the companies sell life insurance to people who can't afford it, don't understand it, or are tricked into giving up an old policy for a new one. At a rough estimate, lapses cost the people who drop the insurance about $10,000,000,-000 worth of insurance protection a year and about $2,000,-000,000 in out-of-pocket losses.

That's one by-product of the way the industry is run.*

Then, out of every five insurance policies purchased, only one matures as a death claim. Somewhere along the line, the other four go by the board. Many policies mature when their owners turn them in for their cash value. But many more are "twisted" off the books by agents who use the cash values to pay premiums on new policies.

You can argue that an industry which wastes a quarter of its energy on sales it shouldn't be making is poorly managed. You can conclude correctly that life insurance is a travesty of the philanthropic public service its leaders say it is. You can realize that the promises held out to you by these leaders are hollow.

But it doesn't matter what you think. The courteous, religious gentlemen who run the industry plan to go on running it just the way they always have. After all, they say, lapse ratios of 25 per cent have been the rule for seventy-five years. We can't change human nature.

However, these men could teach their agents first to sell life insurance properly and then to provide genuine service to the customer. Other American industries, even such direct-to-customer enterprises as the vacuum-cleaner and kitchenware hawkers—have learned to do as much. But you'll wait a long time before the life insurance industry fulfills its obligations of "lifetime service."

The industry isn't controlled by a gang of thieves and corporate plunderers in the grand style. The last thing life insurance officials need to do is rob us; the legal use of our money gives them all the leverage they want. The fact that these officials occupy high positions is enough to guarantee

---

* For many years, the industry's shriller critics have used lapse-ratio statistics as evidence that life insurance is fraudulent. But it's much more realistic to shift emphasis onto ineptitude and identify this waste of our money with bad management.

them opportunities to get rich; and many of them do get rich—legally. But such opportunists aside, the industry's chieftains are either narrowly specialized bureaucrats or else figureheads, lacking both the larcenous vitality of the corporate buccaneer and the capacity or will of the industrial reformer. Blaming these mediocrities for the wretched state of the industry is like blaming President James Buchanan for the Civil War.

Nevertheless, as we said near the beginning of this chapter, "the buck stops here"—"here" being the palatial executive suites these executives love to build.

Because Americans basically believe in business leadership, we are almost too willing to entrust great power to top management, whether in profit-making corporations like General Motors or in our huge life insurance companies. Because we can exert some measure of control over even the biggest profit-making enterprise, the balance of power is less one-sided than the size and scope of Big Business suggests. But with nobody to account to, and behind all its sententiousness, no true sense of public service, the "non-profit" life insurance industry has betrayed our confidence. Insurance leadership has passed the buck right back to the public.

"The worst-managed Big Business in America."
—*the Consultant*

8 . *The Dim Light of Reform*

THE SAD TRUTHS about the behavior of top management and the entire rueful tale of how the industry operates may dismay you or even confirm your darkest suspicions about life insurance. Such huge-scale wastefulness, inefficiency, and bad management obviously don't come free of charge. On the contrary, you are paying the price. And more to the point, because your insurance dollars aren't buying all that they could be, your wife and children will one day be the poorer.

As we're about to discover, however, the forces of reform are already active within the industry. Unfortunately, the reformers are fighting an uphill battle, and the outcome of their struggle is highly dubious. The advocates of change and improvement are up against more than the massive vested power of the industry itself; they also have their own special problems to contend with. But before we meet the reformers, let's focus briefly on something that in the light of what we know about the industry will seem positively Utopian—that is, precisely what reform could mean to you.

Surely the most important impact of reform would be this: your insurance would cost you a lot less money. (Separately and off the record, five high officials, each representing a different one of the ten largest companies, volunteered that "rates could be reduced by about thirty per cent without affecting operations.") Lower rates would mean that your present investment in life insurance would be worth a great deal more to you and your beneficiaries. If you've ever felt that you simply couldn't afford to do an adequate job of protecting your family, some of your frustration, at least, would evaporate.

But such a revolution in the pricing of life insurance would be only one end result of reform. Assuming that the industry had really committed itself to change, other—and equally incredible—ramifications would also develop. For instance, when you needed insurance advice, you would simply visit or be visited by a trained specialist, a kind of insurance engineer, who really knew something about insurance. This specialist would be paid only to advise and explain; he might not even be licensed as an agent. True, he'd be representing one company out of many. But he would have no personal stake (no commission) in making you follow his suggestions, and it would be primarily up to his company to attract you and retain your loyalty as a customer. This the company could do only by relying on the excellence of its reputation and the quality and diversity of its services (which might include, just for an easy example, other forms of financial-planning assistance).

Having decided to buy insurance, you'd do no more than answer a few brief questions, sign your name to one simple form, get your policy through the mail or where you work, and even have your premiums automatically withdrawn from your salary. In fact, if you had ever bought any life insurance before, the present company might not have to ask you for more than the proper spelling of your name, and you could actually add new insurance to your policy simply by making a telephone call. So the tiresome rituals of listening to some salesman test his skills, of being examined by a company doctor, and of waiting weeks to have your policy delivered—these routines would be gone forever.

Your policies themselves would be different. Arranged in readable form and perhaps even informatively illustrated, they would be written in layman's language, with costs, benefits, limitations, and "extras" made absolutely clear. If you wanted to make a change in an existing policy, all you'd have to do is notify the local branch office of the company (perhaps only giving a clerk your personal code number) and wait while the change was effected. Similarly, over high-speed audio-visual communications circuits, the home office would furnish within minutes any additional information you might happen to want or need.

Finally, new and thought-provoking insurance concepts would first supplement and then entirely replace the present time-worn policies. Permanent insurance that costs little more than today's temporary coverage, "instant" insurance that you could add for a few weeks or months to cover some short-range need, and policies geared to your personal earnings or even to the value of the dollar—such arrangements would be the rule.

Do these innovations sound like daydreams? Perhaps they do. Yet every single one of the products and services just mentioned is either in actual use (on a limited but non-experimental basis) or well within the means, both technical and financial, of today's life insurance industry. Indeed, to many outside experts—including actuaries, management engineers, and economists—such "revolutionary" possibilities already sound old-hat. Right now the real visionaries are debating such ideas as free life insurance from birth to age twenty-one, mass coverage of so-called "uninsurables," and credit schemes that would allow you up to, say, $5,000 worth of free merchandise because insurance on your life would eventually pay the bill.

Thus, contemporary life insurance reformers have on their side the fact that the tools of reform, if not the spirit, are readily available. Before identifying these reformers, however, we must take time to consider one more thing. Or rather, let's make explicit what has been very much implicit throughout this book: there is, and in fact always has been, a great, unresolved ambiguity confronting everybody who has ever had to think about the American life insurance industry. That ambiguity, of course, is whether life insurance is primarily a business, primarily a social institution, or somehow a blend of both.

From the beginning, uncertainty about this riddle has plagued everybody, from the humblest agents and their customers to the mightiest executives, from the industry's own paid chroniclers and philosophers to serious historians and social thinkers. There may be no final answer, or at least none that lies within the scope of this book. But the problem still remains; and just as that problem has confused legislators, officials of other industries, and economists (to mention a few more categories of the puzzled), so does it baffle the reformers. The most important fact to keep in mind about the industry's gadflies is that from their contrasting answers to this business-versus-institution riddle come their contrasting proposals for reform.

First, let's meet the *business-oriented* reformers. As an advocate of (and the leading spokesman for) revitalizing the business end of life insurance, Richard F. Neuschel, our acquaintance from the preceding chapter, is particularly notable. Like so many management consultants, Mr. Neuschel is a technician—almost a metaphysician—of sound corporate practice for its own sake. And as a true devotee should, Mr. Neuschel speaks up loud and clear:

> The driving focus of the whole top-management team must be on seizing every opportunity to provide products or services that customers need and want. The opposite of this sort of consumer orientation is corporate or departmental self-centeredness, which Dimock [Marshall Dimock, a noted authority on management] further refers to as "pathological bureaucracy."

Because Mr. Neuschel speaks from within the business framework, his rebukes carry an insider's forcefulness and logic. And there's no doubt at all about his orientation when he stands before an audience of top life insurance executives and voices a blunt warning:

> You have a responsibility to all the people of our country to demonstrate, *by sheer management excellence and vitality,* that the private enterprise system is incontrovertibly the best method of managing this great industry.

In short, either improve or else face the spectre of government takeover.

However, Mr. Neuschel is much more optimistic than that grim admonition makes him sound. Off the record he even allows himself to speak of a "management revolution" within the life insurance industry and of a coming top-management generation that wants to bring about great changes. In fact, Mr. Neuschel and his fellow consultants seem to have discovered that within life insurance there exists a kind of management underground. In many companies, and perhaps especially in the biggest and most ossified, a handful of young executives are quietly longing for the day when, as top management, they'll really be able to straighten things out.

These Young Turks are mostly administrators, who have earnestly enough been trying to streamline the clumsy routines of home-office management. Among them are members of a new and rarefied breed, executives who really do understand computers and their application. As a classic case of what these insiders can do, take the young specialist who was helping his company's service staff process the list of all the company's policy owners into the transistorized memory of a new computer. During the operation this executive discovered that 40 per cent of the new policies sold each year were repeat sales to people who had bought from the company earlier. He further learned that most of those repeat sales were made by a small minority (about 15 per cent) of the sales force. Knowing that such facts have heavy implications, he took his findings to the sales vice-president, who told him sourly to "quit trying to show us how to run the Sales Department."

Undiscouraged, our bright young man began running various special policy-owner lists through his computer, classifying and cross-checking their statistical patterns against his previous information. Finally, he did come up with an interesting set of figures. Business resulting from "leads" (coupon-ad replies, calls from customers whose agents were no longer around, and other requests for help) lagged far behind the category of sales to previous customers. He soon learned that the Sales Department was giving the leads to new agents as part of their training program.

"We're losing business by giving new men these leads," he protested; and he finally persuaded the Sales Department to turn over leads only to experienced agents. As a result, sales from leads *trebled* in one year. And this young man, who has never actually sold an insurance policy in his life, brought nearly $10,000,000 worth of new life insurance onto the books.

To management planners like Richard Neuschel, this kind of executive enterprise could obviously make a great difference. Such experts sincerely believe that a more efficient use of existing resources is the true answer to reforming the life insurance industry. Thus, the consultants and their allies among the Young Turks set great store by modernization of office methods. They talk about revamping underwriting and investment practices. They'd like to make effective use of advanced cost-control and forward-planning techniques. They correspond with other theorists of administration in both business and government, and a few of them even dabble in games theory and other simulation systems of business strategy.

Quite a few of these outside consultants are even prepared to reshape the ideas and attitudes of industry leadership. These experts make no bones about the need for "tautening up the management structure." According to one consultant, "You'd never believe how many middle-aged men with severe disabilities are clogging the top floor in most big life companies. Why, one of my clients has two vice-presidents who haven't done a stroke of real work in years. One of them is an alcoholic; the other's got bad heart trouble. But just for showing up at the office, the first guy draws fifty thousand dollars a year and the second makes over thirty-five thousand." To us, the executive "loyalty" that leads to featherbedding on such a scale may be a particularly rank abuse of privilege. To the consultants, however, it's something different and even worse. It's a sin against efficient management.

Of the ten biggest life companies, at least three are now

worried enough about their problems to be paying big yearly retainers to management-consultant firms. From the public record there's no way of knowing how many other major companies have also brought in the McKinseys and the Booz Allen & Hamiltons to help. But industry gossip indicates that many have and that even more are very quietly signing long-term contracts with these professional outsiders.

In such a trend you may see signs that the industry is at long last beginning to bestir itself. Even though you recall that life insurance management has long made a fad of using consultants (for example, in "agent education" and "communications"), you may feel that the big-time professionals are likely to be taken seriously. But before reaching that optimistic conclusion, you should ask yourself whether or not even the most dedicated consultant *can* reach the heart of this industry's problems. In short, is a Richard Neuschel really able to push hard enough to produce a meaningful change?

An ominous hint, not of Mr. Neuschel's personal limitations but of those imposed on any consultant, is contained in another recent speech he has made before an important industry group (September, 1965). Mr. Neuschel stated, as firmly as always: "Sales manpower development . . . is the key to marketing vitality—not product design, not price, not advertising, not sales promotion, and not any of the other marketing tools that are so important to other industries." If you've come to believe that precisely those "other tools"— decent advertising, public relations, and communications— should become the most potent weapons of reform, you can't help feeling that here Mr. Neuschel has suddenly begun to talk like just another life insurance official. (True, following this speech, a McKinsey & Company colleague of Neuschel's, Phillip Dutter, introduced to the same audience a rather novel idea—for life insurance men anyway. Dutter insisted that hiring superior sales *managers* is the best guarantee of getting and keeping good agents, a thesis that Neuschel himself entirely supports. But the point is that both men join in downgrading the importance of every facet of life insurance except one—direct sales.)

So though they speak out strongly, the consultants are certainly not what you would call revolutionaries of life insurance. The probing of surgeons like Dutter and Neuschel may well strike some sensitive nerves. But ever since 1878, when Elizur Wright published *Traps Baited with Orphan,* the industry has had opportunities to ignore criticism from within. Moreover, as we'll be asking ourselves again later, does the promise or even the achievement of the consultant's dream of "good management" really solve the industry's problems or our own?

Leaving that question for the moment, let's make room for a second group of specialists interested in reform. This group doesn't talk the businessese of the good-management team, but uses instead a convoluted language of its own, that of the social sciences. For that's what the second group is: a circle, still small but growing rapidly, of academic sociologists, psychologists, and anthropologists, all on occasion preoccupied with life insurance.

Actually, there is considerable precedent for a link between the behavioral sciences and the insurance industry. As long ago as 1913, Haley Fiske, Metropolitan Life's chief executive, hired Dr. Louis I. Dublin to head an Industrial Research Department for the company. Primarily an authority on public health, Dr. Dublin also turned out to be something of a pioneer in social science. Under his influence the Metropolitan acquired an almost paternal interest in the social well-being of its immense clientele. (During the 1920's, for instance, Haley Fiske himself tried to interest the entire industry in underwriting a private unemployment insurance scheme. But to no avail.)

Logically enough, the industry's selection and actuarial wing has always been in close contact with the social sciences. As a prime source of raw data about the American public's living habits and health, the industry has both issued its own studies and made information available to outside scholars. Moreover, as a center of research in statistical mathematics, the life insurance industry has indirectly benefited the statisticians of social science.

But aside from such narrowly technical interchanges, nobody in top management had, until the past few years, paid much attention to what everyone else recognized as a spectacular explosion in the science of society. Almost the only attempt to put life insurance leaders in touch with the new world of behavioral study virtually died in childbirth. A decade ago a Chicago advertising man (and motivation-research advocate), Edward H. Weiss, tried to sell a group of life insurance advertisers on becoming "hidden persuaders." Weiss had commissioned a "psychological depth study" of "Hidden Attitudes Toward Life Insurance," and used the study's findings in support of his views that life insurance advertising was all wrong. But though this analysis did contain some sensitive insights into the psychology of insurance buyers and sellers, Weiss's ideas created no more than a ripple of interest (Vance Packard mentions the incident in *The Hidden Persuaders*). In 1955 this industry's sales executives simply weren't up to accepting psychoanalytic techniques as a basis for consumer research or advertising. Now, eleven years later, most of them still aren't.

Thus, the upsurge of interest in modern social science is

really no more than a few years old. We can date the new era from 1960, when former utilities magnate James F. Oates became the new president of Equitable Life. Among the many questions this chief executive from outside asked his new subordinates at the Equitable was, "Where's our research and development?" His associates at first looked at him blankly and finally directed him to the actuarial division. But Oates, no ordinary life insurance leader, had something completely different in mind. Life insurance, he maintained, is a business of people; and therefore, in the life insurance business, research and development means research into human behavior, and thus the study of men, their institutions, value systems and ideologies.

Fortunately, Oates had the right personal connections to begin a careful search for what he wanted, an academic social scientist willing to put his special skills to work for the Equitable. At first he confined that search to the Ivy League, trying Princeton and then Harvard. (Harvard sent down a special task force of professors on a related errand, to explore the company's operations and then report their findings. This the professors did—in five thick volumes.) Finally, Columbia University's noted sociologist Robert K. Merton suggested John W. Riley, Jr., then head of the Department of Sociology at Rutgers University.

Dr. Merton and Dr. Riley were old Army buddies, members of a sociological research team that during World War II had helped the Army conduct its Special Operations (i.e., psychological warfare) program. According to an informant, another sociologist, "Guys like Riley and Merton were the ones who first sold everybody—in government, industry, and every place else—on 'applied' social science."

At Merton's and Oates's urging, Dr. Riley overcame his

reluctance to leave Rutgers, and in 1961 he accepted an appointment as Second Vice-President and Director of Social Research for the Equitable.

Because Riley was a key member of the Social Science Establishment, his appointment almost automatically focused the attention of academic sociology and its behavioral-science relatives onto life insurance. Riley figuratively brought with him to the Equitable an extremely influential segment of the academic community, a segment, moreover, that Riley has kept actively vocal about life insurance.

"If there has ever been a time when we have arrogantly separated ourselves from the rest of the community, then that time must be over once and for all," Riley maintains. Professorial dignity hasn't kept him from being pungent on the subject of the industry's shortcomings, but his is a different brand of pepperiness than that of Richard Neuschel, for Riley isn't primarily interested in applying the scalpel to top management. Instead, he's much more concerned with (and like a good scientist, curious about) the relationships and the gaps between the industry as a social institution and the various aggregations of people who surround it, penetrate it, and react to it. To Riley and his colleagues, the malfunctioning of life insurance is largely due to its inwardness (Neuschel called it "corporate self-centeredness"). Change, therefore, carries the special meaning of "opening up" and communicating.

In addition to addressing itself to policyholders, agents, investors, doctors, lawmakers, beneficiaries, suppliers, home-owners, and countless other specialized publics, [a large mutual life insurance company] must also concern itself with its proper role in the complex areas of health and safety, education, research, community welfare, employment practices, urban planning, social legislation, and dozens of other highly important and vital issues which are so characteristic of the larger society within which it operates.

This statement, from *The Corporation and Its Publics: Essays on the Corporate Image,* a book Riley edited for the Foundation for Research into Human Behavior, is a manifesto of the reform he advocates. To Riley, not only communication but active engagement in the work of the community seems the *sine qua non* for a big corporation. That the Equitable is willing to encourage and even subsidize such talk is something of a victory in advance for Riley, whose ideas far outrange the usual industry ideas about public relations.

> The mere creation of an image for projection to the public-at-large will not obviate the need to communicate to those special publics, nor will it solve the problem of how the company is to define the range of its social responsibilities.

You expect to find IBM or Standard Oil thus trying to broaden the domain of public relations and corporate responsibilities. Within the life insurance framework this sophisticated appraisal of the need for active communication and participation seems like a fresh, cool breeze.

As a human link in the Equitable's still tenuous communications network, Riley's efforts and contacts have enabled him to do such things as put together a special issue of *The American Behavioral Scientist* (May, 1963) subtitled *Social Research and Life Insurance.* True, that particular attempt to communicate about communication contained a great deal of padding. Industry executives were given space to utter such profundities as "Insurance in its broadest sense is an 'instinctive' act of self-reliance," and—on the need for research—"It is better to light one candle than to curse the darkness." But the issue also carried articles of serious in-

terest by such leading social scientists as Kingsley Davis of
the University of California and Talcott Parsons of Harvard.
There was even a contribution, "Time, the Ultimate Scar-
city," by Wilbert E. Moore, author of the provocative *Man,
Time, and Society.* In short, Riley's act of assembling the
issue was also an effort at rehabilitation, an attempt, as
Riley himself put it, "to make life insurance a respectable
subject for intellectuals." Again, when you consider how this
industry feels about communicating, his achievement was
almost the equivalent of the first flight at Kitty Hawk.

To most insurance men, such an attempt, like much else
that Riley tries to do, is as remote as the moon. But in 1964
Riley (with the backing of Oates and many of the trustees)
sponsored one move at the Equitable that not only attracted
the attention of the rest of the industry, but in one public
relations man's words, "scared the hell out of it." Riley
urged that the Equitable take the strongest possible *public*
stand on civil rights. And late in the year the Equitable's
sales-recruiting ads began to carry the tag line, "An Equal
Opportunity Employer."

As you already know, the life insurance industry has hoped
all along that the Negro's struggle for equal rights would go
away if only everybody kept quiet. So the Equitable's decision profoundly shocked the industry's top management.
And when, in the trade press and in such Negro magazines
as *Ebony*, the company began running ads that actually
showed a Negro agent selling insurance to a white couple,
the turmoil in the executive suites became feverish. Moreover, Riley made the Equitable's position perfectly clear
when he said, "We feel that being a good corporate citizen
means taking the proper stand on certain social issues. It
was time for someone in this industry to declare that discrimination against Negroes is bad and stupid. And when

other public issues also reach a critical stage, we'll be taking positions on them, too."

Riley knew perfectly well that this matter-of-fact approach was the best possible way to dramatize the Equitable's "new" attitude. It takes nothing away from the validity of the civil rights stand to point out that the Equitable has thousands of Negro policy owners (and prospective customers), or that this strong declaration gave the company a real public relations edge over the rest of the industry. (Not until a full year later did a second major company, the Metropolitan, decide to follow in the Equitable's footsteps. Now, one more company at a time, you can expect most of the industry to plod slowly into line.)

Aside from being a critical social and moral issue, civil rights has given Riley a kind of test situation, one that reflects his own and his colleagues' broadest concerns. Within our culture, the social scientists are saying, the most important social institutions are governmental and *business* entities. Businesses have definite social obligations and responsibilities. For a given company to supply some socially valuable product or service—whether automobiles, color TV, or life insurance—is no longer enough to discharge those obligations. Since every big business leaves indelible marks on society, business leadership cannot either deny or ignore the need to harmonize the special goals of private enterprise with society's best interests.

According to the way social scientists read events, business today must even be prepared to nurse the ailing segments of our society. A healthy social order is management's only guarantee of future markets and profits; therefore, business will have to make increasing commitments of money and time to help people solve their private difficulties and their social problems. This means dealing with people not merely as members of abstract categories ("customers," "stock-holders," "officials"), but as human beings in all their complexity. In short, now modern business must do what earlier businesses would not and could not do: take on the contemporary equivalent of what one of Riley's colleagues calls "vaccinating the buffalo and irrigating the prairie."

For a long time sophisticated corporations have been saying, and in some ways doing, precisely this sort of thing. The question is, will Riley and his friends be able to convince more of the life insurance industry of the urgent importance of this corporate sociology? Only if these social scientists keep on making news and attracting executive support will they have much chance of pushing this industry into an important role in the conservation of human resources.

We've glanced at two separate reform movements: one that wants life insurance to be a more efficient *business* and another that wants to make the industry into a better *social* institution. Both camps obviously have plausible ideas to recommend and talented specialists to help put those ideas to work. In very different ways, moreover, both sets of reformers have a good deal of glamour to offer this notably unglamorous industry. We might have fun speculating what would happen if top management suddenly decided to dose itself with both kinds of remedies at once.

But given today's life insurance industry, we know only too well that such a day is hardly likely to dawn in the near future. And unfortunately, the industry's built-in resistance to change isn't the main reason why the Neuschels on the one hand and the Rileys on the other are going to have tough sledding. A much more basic reason is that the programs, speeches, seminars, symposia, journals, and other activities of the reformers all have in common a terrible, disturbing remoteness from this industry's daily reality. At this point the reformers just don't have in focus what is the real problem in life insurance.

According to every scrap of evidence, that problem is the enormous sum total of our own individual problems—of everybody's problems—in dealing with the life insurance agent. As we've seen, the good-management-oriented reformers naturally think that good management will help. The social scientists are only now beginning to study the salesman and the Agency System. But thus far *nobody* has dared to say the obvious: Americans no longer need or want the American Agency System.

Recently someone has come close to this verdict, someone whom even life insurance officials must respect. David Ogilvy is one of the most brilliant advertising men in the country precisely because he began as a salesman (of stoves and other appliances, door to door). Speaking as a master of the sales trade, Ogilvy (whose agency has sold everything from Rolls-Royces to breakfast food) said quietly in a speech to the Life Insurance Agency Management Association (November, 1965):

> It seems to me that the future of most life insurance companies, as they are now set up, depends on whether you can persuade enough good men that selling insurance is a worthwhile career.
>
> I don't think you can.

But concerned as he is about this probably fatal shortage of salesmen, even Mr. Ogilvy side-steps the main point. We undoubtedly do want our insurance explained and prescribed by experts. We certainly also want to know more about life insurance and how it can help us. But most of us would be only too grateful if our insurance could be *supplied* as automatically and impersonally as banking and allied money services are now supplied.

Today the fact, the logic, and the spirit of our culture all point in this one direction. For instance, consider the overwhelming commitment our society has made to such indirectly purchased benefits as those of Social Security and other government welfare programs. Note that our demands are fostering incredibly rapid growth in such "automatic insurance" as employee group coverage and credit life insurance. After a spirited beginning, Ogilvy suddenly stopped short and said to his audience, "I am not suggesting that you abolish the agency [salesman] system overnight. Perish forbid." But the truth about life insurance distribution today is that the American Agency System is a bottleneck. *It may even be keeping Americans from buying an incalculably greater amount of insurance than is now being sold.*

Don't forget that this system was designed for the horse-and-buggy era and that its growth has never been planned, but has come about strictly as a matter of expediency. When you consider how inept the average insurance salesman is, how badly trained, how awkward and self-conscious, you may well believe that he loses sales right and left. And finally, ask yourself whether 500,000 men, many of them part-time shock troops, can really take care of the *genuine* insurance needs of 200,000,000 Americans.

Then you'll see why life insurance reform doesn't begin with "improvement" of the Agency System, any more than human evolution began with the improvement of the dinosaur. Nor does reform involve the transformation of that system into a more modern sales-and-service organization. Reform really begins—and why *not* now?—with the abolition of the life insurance agent and the removal of that dead weight, the Agency System.

Contrary to the throat-clearing, toe-scuffing, and righteous indignation of the Agency System's bigwigs, a program to eliminate the system is simple to design and put into effect. First of all, such a program would curb the autonomy of the agency manager, who must no longer be allowed to get rich by dishonest recruitment and outright thievery from his agents. His agency must be made into a true company branch office, under constant surveillance by home-office management. His salesmen must be turned into salaried employees, for then and only then can the company demand steady eight-hour-a-day performance and offer rewards other than the treadmill. Such men can be hired much more selectively (perhaps through field personnel offices that will finally turn those tests into something meaningful), given limited but firm tenure, and trained to be of real service to the public.

Because these field men won't be there primarily to sell, the company itself must begin to attract customers by using such techniques as effective direct mail (one of Mr. Ogilvy's pet ideas), intelligent advertising, and faithful attention to old customers. Even more important, a combination of modern insurance products and old-fashioned price lowering will keep sales levels high. A 15 per cent slash in rates would do more for the sales curve and for the customer than this industry has done since 1900.

By now our intimate knowledge of the Agency System tells us that its dismantling should certainly be a project dear to both management-oriented and sociological reformers. How often does anyone get the chance not only to rid an industry of its most inefficient operation but also to help restore the industry to membership in society? Reformers of any stripe could respond to the challenge of rebuilding life insurance distribution. Either side could also revivify the industry's top management. Carrying out a phase-by-phase program without losing sales is a project that could transform the industry's home offices into exciting business environments.

The farewell to the Agency System might only be a beginning. Perhaps a re-examination of the concepts underlying life insurance could come next. Take, for example, the variable annuity, an insurance contract that makes some controversial departures from traditional policy forms. In the variable annuity, the owner develops a retirement fund based in part on conventional "fixed dollar" investments and guarantees and in part on stock portfolio values. At present, variable annuities are in their infancy. If the industry decided in earnest to push the variable annuity, the nature of life insurance could change radically. Insurance companies could broaden their services to include investment counseling, and do so on a gigantic scale.

Even to consider such changes, this industry will definitely have to reconsider its stand on the question of state-versus-federal regulation. For life insurance to catch up with the times, the lobbyists will have to take the offensive and campaign to widen the legal base on which insurance now rests. Despite its fear of being taxed to death, life insurance leadership must realize that a federally regulated industry might in fact be freer to change its products and services than will ever be the case under state supervision. And as an aide to the Senate Finance Committee made clear, "If they want to talk, we're willing to listen."

We have already envisioned some of the consequences of reform. We should also make one final comment. When the processes of change really begin to work within a huge institution, the final results are unpredictable, and this industry is based on man's ability to predict. But if top management will only take up the challenge, then change—an infusion of outside blood into management, for instance—will recharge the life insurance industry. Furthermore, in this generation management could take credit for a revolution without becoming the revolution's first victims. If, on the other hand, life insurance management ignores its opportunities, the industry's brass hats will learn the lesson that other drowsing business giants have learned. As one commentator has noted, "If the railroads had realized their business was transportation and not just rolling stock, today they'd own the airlines."

"Would You Pay a Hundred Dollars a Year to Live
Forever?"
—*title of a Sales Talk*

9 . Life, Death, and Money: Our American Immortality Syndrome

"AFTER ALL, we're selling a billion dollars' worth of insurance every single year. We must be doing *something* right." Whether the industry that sells us our life insurance is doing something right, something wrong, or just *something* is a question we've been arguing steadily throughout this book. Nevertheless, this utterance (the words of yet another life insurance executive) is a perfect introduction to a chapter that first asks and then gives some answers to a new question: Why do we *really* buy life insurance?

This question certainly isn't answered by the maudlin phrases of the insurance ads ("Because You Really Care— a Special Gift") or by the eager sincerity your agent exudes so strongly. On the contrary, we must look for an answer in theories which to most insurance men will seem to be written in a tongue unknown.

To people from other countries, our life insurance habits seem strange, even exotic. According to a French businessman who learned about the American insurance industry during a lengthy stay in New York, "You people are insurance-crazed. In France a man grows up, gets married, has children, and becomes middle-aged before he even *thinks* about insuring his life. Then maybe he buys a little policy —enough to pay for a funeral. He *buys* it, mind you. If one of your agents came to a Frenchman, he'd get thrown out on his ear.

"But in the States everybody buys insurance—children, young women, even the cats and dogs. What do you want to spend all that money for?"

And even though England originated modern life insurance, the English also regard us as slightly demented on the subject. One young man, here on a training mission for a London life insurance company, was flabbergasted at the casual way Americans undertake insurance programs. "I called on one chap—you know, just knocked on his door— and the next thing, he had me inside and was telling me the entire story of his life. Everything about his salary, his bank account, what he spent, that sort of thing. Inside of one hour he signed up to pay fifteen-hundred dollars a year for a policy with me—a total stranger. The *last* thing anyone in England would do."

For us, life insurance is surely something more than a product we buy or even an institution with peculiar folkways of its own. Because that $100,000,000,000 worth of insurance a year is such a staggering amount and its purchase so important a fact of our lives, we should think about life insurance as an American social phenomenon. But to do this, we need to see ourselves and our insurance in a fresh perspective. We need some anthropological measuring rods.

When a cultural anthropologist examines any society, one of his best strategies is to decode that society's attitudes toward certain human universals. The most familiar example of the impact of such a universal on society is probably that in every society so far studied, the entire order of things is ranged against incest. Whether you're on a field trip in the rain forests of South America or wandering across town to look at the social habits of your nearer neighbors, you can take for granted that the incest taboo is a standard against which every society adjusts its own sexual, marital, and inter-family relationships.

In contrast, of course, other universals inspire an incredibly wide range of attitudes and behavior among different societies. For instance, consider the fact of aging. Some impoverished cultures take no care whatever of their old people. When the individual grows too old to be active in gathering food, his days of usefulness are over; he is simply allowed to die. Other tribes, however, can afford to cherish their aged members. Their graybeards become chiefs, and social life may in fact organize itself around serving and placating the tribe's senior citizens. But in any case, the given society's reaction to aging and to old age is crucially important for the society's survival and prosperity. To understand the society at all the anthropologist must understand that reaction. Therefore, he'll hunt for traces of social attitudes toward aging in even the tiniest nuances of behavior.

Moreover, in what the society itself accepts as most natural, the trained observer will find his most revealing clues. For example, when we Americans eat, we practice extremely elaborate, ritualistic patterns of behavior. In fact, you could base a lengthy doctoral dissertation on such minute detail as our use of the napkin. The whole point of your study would be to illustrate that in our own culture, eating has taken on an importance far beyond what is required for the efficient ingestion of food. And you would have to conclude that food and eating are of central, and maybe even of supreme, importance and significance to modern Western society.

Let's apply a similar approach to another mainstay of Western (and specifically American) society—money. Further, let's see what clues to our attitudes about money are contained in the great mirror of any society's feelings and thoughts—language. There is something especially curious and revealing about certain sets of synonyms for money that keep cropping up in our daily language.

In various contexts we call money dough, the long green, a potful, and most starkly, bread. Two vegetable synonyms that immediately come to mind are lettuce and cabbage. Obviously, we do associate money with food. Less obviously, however, we talk about money specifically in terms of the foods we grow and cultivate. Indeed, though money may not grow on trees, we still call it bananas and hope that money falls when we shake the plum tree.

In the special vocabularies of business and finance we find many more examples of this curious kind of "agrarian" money imagery. Investors talk about seed money, about raking it in and then ploughing back the profits. We hear of fruitful investments and flourishing (i.e., flowering) enterprises. Deals are juicy, opportunities are ripe for the picking, and money ain't hay. Businessmen also speak of money as if it were a domestic animal; they harness assets, tie up funds, and put money to work. Furthermore, they take good care of that nest egg.

An anthropologist might only comment that even in a highly industrialized age we still talk about money as if we were still farmers and gardeners. He might deduce that as reflected in such language, our feelings about money are indeed conservative and old-fashioned. But in this way of talking about money, a poet might see the association between

186·

this agrarian vocabulary and the idea of growth and increase. In short, we link money with fertility.

Another intriguing set of synonyms for money clusters around water. Money is liquid. Unless the assets are frozen, funds flow. Money accumulates in pools and reservoirs, pours into investments, trickles down to the workers, or lies stagnant. A bad investment soaks up money like a sponge. Even highly specialized vocabularies rely on such imagery. Economists talk about levels of spending and saving. Businessmen take advantage of spill-over subsidiary deals, and for their wealthy clients, lawyers design pour-over trusts and guarantee the fluidity of estates.

Here, too, the anthropologist might point out that such a set of synonyms is a cultural anachronism, a holdover from an agrarian age now past. And he'd be right. But the poet's sensitivity to language would tell him that we identify money with water and both in turn with the idea of transformation and change. Like water, which liquefies and dissolves even rock, money is an agent of change; in fact, the medium of exchange.

We could go on indefinitely, developing these almost-Shakespearean sets and clusters of money synonyms. (For a fascinating final example, note the use of marine, and specifically submarine, words for the bad or unfavorable aspects of money. Like a bad investment, a man who cadges money is a sponge; and the money itself is down the drain. A usurer, on the other hand, is a loan shark or bloodsucker, and a big-money interest is an octopus.) But now let's shift to another set of synonyms, those that have to do with *spending* money. Strangely, one cluster of synonyms for spending is related to the idea of removing the clothes. You divest yourself of funds, you strip your pockets, you unbelt, you loosen up, you unbutton your purse. Even more interesting is the vitality of the verbs we use to describe the act of spending. You throw money around (or away), you spread it, you blow your pay check, you lay money on (lend it to) a buddy or lay it on the line, you shoot the wad. Similarly, when you've got a lot of money, you're not only wealthy, but loaded with potential energy; in fact, you're loaded. You're flush. Like uranium, the money's burning a hole in your pocket; you've got an itch to paper the town with it.

One particularly evocative way to see how we feel about spending is to remember that we naturally think of the big spender as a physically big man. Rarely, if ever, do we associate free spending with the mousy, balding, bespectacled fellow. On the contrary, *he's* the bookkeeper, who never spends a dime if he can help it. The prototype of the American big spender, the fast man with a buck, is the Texan, the Big Daddy who stands six-five in his hand-tooled boots and flashes a roll that, interestingly enough, would choke a horse.

By now the point should be clear. In our society money has always been a primary symbol of life itself. We associate money with growth and change, with the great benevolent life-giving forces: food, water, the fertile soil. Indeed, to us, money has a life of its own. Like a second soul, money is physically part of us: something can cost an arm and a leg; the loan shark demands his pound of flesh. Especially in today's consumption-minded society, buying things with money is symbolically nothing less than the very act of giving life. According to whole institutes of psychologists (and to the advertising experts, who are paid well to understand such things), spending money is the symbolic equivalent of spending semen, the economic counterpart of the virile, potent, masculine creative act.

Because in countless ways we equate money with life, we

shouldn't wonder that there's a strong compulsion to buy off death itself with money.

Here we come to a turning point. For the time being we must direct our thoughts away from money and toward the topic of death, particularly in American society. No human universal has meant so much, and so many different things, as our foreknowledge that we must die.

In some societies the dead have laid so strong a claim that the living have organized themselves into living memorials, devoted only to serving the dead. Ancient Egypt is the classic example of the mortuary culture; but there are others, so numerous that we know primitive peoples feel themselves free to live only in the eye of death. We know, too, about man's world-embracing systems of myth, which tell us that along with the precognition of death, men have always felt an anguished psychic yearning for some form of immortality. And seemingly in all men everywhere, that yearning has been one with the fierce need to perceive pattern and meaning in the cosmos. Thus, we have the most wonderful myth of all, that of rebirth, renewal, the eternal return. In Western culture the Christian fulfillment of that myth was for centuries the shaping spirit.

To devout Christians, life itself once meant only the acceptance of and preparation for death. And yet, in Western society, the recent history of death has been the story of the break with that tradition. To digest the gradual transformation of attitudes toward death first in Europe and later in America is impossible, like trying to cram into one book the separate histories of religion, philosophy, literature, art, medicine, science, technology, and political and social revolution since 1650. However, for a host of reasons, historians and social scientists are telling us that in modern times death has more and more lost its significance. It has come to mean simply the final incident in life. To some commentators, this change represents the triumph of life over death. To others, the contemporary attitude toward death implies only that some necessary sense of limitation to our lives has been misplaced.

But if there really is any such thing as a "triumph" of life over death, we have seen it happen in our own society, and in an endless number of ways we are celebrating that same victory every day. Instead of building pyramids or cathedrals, we erect skyscrapers. Our heroes are the young "beautiful people"; we are said to worship children. Although our land frontiers have been closed for three quarters of a century, we still like to believe that we are an ageless, growing culture, and so we thrust forth into space. Moreover, by applying to some kinds of death the same efficient, organized effort we apply to so much of life, we have indeed miraculously succeeded in pushing death away. Today we may be on the brink of substantially lengthening the span of life and perhaps even of fabricating life in our laboratories. In such a burgeoning, pulsing society there seems to be no room left for death.

And yet there must be room. Every year 2,000,000 of us die. (In 1963 the exact figure was 1,813,549.) True, 4,000,-000 Americans are born each year (which is what we mean by a population explosion). But nevertheless, in any given year, one out of every hundred Americans dies. Death is surely no alien to our society. Where death is concerned, why are our customs what they are?

For a long time outsiders have had a field day with American attitudes toward death. Europeans in particular seem to delight in accusing American society of harboring silly, crude, and dangerous notions about death. To the French, for instance, we are precisely what our worst movies say we are:

a nation of gangsters and brawlers who commonly settle disputes with gun, switchblade, or blackjack. Our police are themselves legal criminals, our cities morasses of crime, our highways motorized killing grounds, and so on and on and on. In the Frenchman's U.S.A., life is cheap, and violent death almost a certainty.

Similarly, the British have made a specialty out of labeling our attitudes toward death grotesque and absurd. Evelyn Waugh's *The Loved One* and Jessica Mitford's *The American Way of Death* point the finger of British wit at our funerary practices. Decades ago Aldous Huxley painted his own grisly picture of a rich American in search of immortality in *After Many a Summer Dies the Swan.*

To pile up evidence that our way of death is bizarre, the British have all gone West to the same place, California. So, for that matter, have any number of celebrated American writers who expound on death; for example, F. Scott Fitzgerald, Nathaniel West, and Terry Southern. California of the sunny skies, balmy climate, and even balmier faddists, eccentrics, and cults is in fact a rich mother lode of matter for mortuary satire.

We may protest that the California realm of Wurlitzerized "memorial gardens" is hardly typical of American thinking about death. Yet the cemetery business, not to mention the funeral industry, thrives nation-wide. No matter what we say, the sound of the electric carillon drowns out our words; and the whole routine of the fancy casket, the prettified corpse, the Cadillac hearse, and the mechanized graveyard makes our denials unconvincing.

Americans may not be either afraid of death or—what our critics would have us admit—unwilling to accept it as part of reality. But nonetheless, in our society, death is a neglected and dispirited institution. Seemingly, we are too preoccupied with life to search for any meaning in death. Like busy executives who have learned to delegate authority, we place death in the hands of specialists: doctors, ministers, undertakers. Then, satisfied that this particular department of society is adequately staffed and well-enough run, we turn our attention elsewhere.

As far as it goes, such an account of our treatment of death tells some significant truths. Taken by itself, death does seem shabby and meaningless in America. But the revealing fact is that Americans don't take death by itself. On the contrary, by every means at our disposal we try to do the exact opposite, to incorporate death into life.

To start with a crucial instance, let's briefly re-examine the American funeral. In *The American Way of Death*, Jessica Mitford focused on an industry and its practices; she shrewdly avoided generalization and let her facts express her viewpoint. But we ourselves have to go at least one step beyond Miss Mitford; for with all its macabre overtones, the American funeral does fulfill successfully a definite social function, to help the living physically surround and thereby keep among themselves the dead.

That our funeral establishments are called homes, or even parlors, is no accident. At funerals we are meant to encounter the dead under circumstances of considerable intimacy, in a crowd of subdued but still lively people. We're supposed to pay our last respects in exactly the same way that we greet the host at a party, politely but informally. The deceased, for the last time, is "At Home" to us. Even the quasi-theatrical tricks of the undertaker's trade—dressing the dead in street clothes or embalming lightly to preserve a life-like appearance—are only efforts to obliterate the borderline between death and life.

The least-noticed but strangest thing about funerals is that the very tastelessness and ordinariness of their atmosphere makes them enough like life (familiar, boringly domestic, and ugly) to be acceptable as an aspect of it. And by this aspect of life we're not meant to be moved or frightened so much as resigned. That's why the one word we use over and over again to describe funerals is "meaningless." In the sense of avoiding any special, disturbing significance, funerals are precisely without meaning.

Some features of what Miss Mitford staunchly refused to call "The High Cost of Leaving" (see her introduction) actually serve a vital purpose of their own. True, funerals are *expensive*—certainly out of proportion to the tangible services rendered. But it's even more interesting that funerals involve rather *complicated* financial transactions, surely much more complicated than the situation calls for. With apologies to Miss Mitford, there is every reason to believe that we want it (or in some sense need it) that way. This familiar challenge of choosing, bargaining, and finally paying money lends to death a touch of life.

We are even told that the dying themselves feel more than anything the need to help the living along. The folklore of hospitals accepts this as a commonplace. One sensitive physician, whose specialty (radiotherapy for cancer) naturally brings him many terminal cases, remarked, "When most of my patients accept that they're going to die, they spend so much of their last time and strength cheering up their families that they don't even notice what's happening to them." According to a hospital nurse, such a reaction is good medicine for the dying patient. "It gives him something to *do*."

The big question for the friends and relatives of a dying man is, Does he know? Should we tell him? We spend a lot of time agonizing over this problem. But our instincts—or at least some very strong social reflexes—advise us to keep quiet. Even though it may mean playing a cruel charade with the victim, we do favor sparing him the knowledge that his time is short. The idea that he has a right to know is alien. We obviously want to avoid liquidating the small amount of life capital he has left, and we want to keep our comrade in the land of the living. To tell him of his impending death, we feel, may tip the balance against him and against ourselves. Death, not life, would then take control.

Just as we feel we must press life upon the dead and dying, so do we carry death back into life by our acts of mourning. To some observers, mourning seems a neglected observance in this society. But despite what such students of our ways say, we do mourn our dead. In some ways, moreover, our mourning is as formal and ceremonious as that of societies where the bereaved wear black, retire from life, and set aside a time to weep.

For us, the real act of homage to the dead is to keep on going. Our funeral games are the full schedule and the uninterrupted daily round. As one newly bereft widow said, "If he can stand to die, I can stand to live," and very soon after the funeral she began accepting social invitations. Indeed, in American society, mourning sometimes takes the form of a kind of suttee in reverse. Instead of seeking a flaming death alongside her deceased husband, many a widow flings herself back into life, using as her self-justification the classic formula, "He would have wanted it that way."

Such mourning in reverse is also a ritual test of endurance, a deliberately Spartan demonstration of our ability to carry someone else's death with us into our own life. In "going on as if nothing had happened," there is the unmistakable sense of participating in a preordained rite. We behave almost like those people in primitive societies who believe that the "life force" of the dead enters into a close relative. In order to preserve that life force intact, such peoples insist upon continuing their own lives. If they should stop life in order to weep, they imperil the soul of the deceased.

Just as we place a kind of *taboo* on overt demonstrations of grief, so do we also restrict talk about our own death. Here, too, we behave like more primitive societies, whose members always believe strongly in the magic potential of language. To name a thing is to evoke it, so it's better not to speak of your death. Furthermore, we suspect that talking too much somehow opens, instead of closing, the gap between life and death. But that we choose to be taciturn about this subject doesn't mean Americans never mention it or think about it. Rather, we feel that there are much better ways than mere conversation to bring death before us.

By what it actually does, any society justifies and tests its attitudes to confirm their validity. With that anthropological truth in mind, we can hardly glance at ourselves without recognizing at once how Americans really feel about death. For in going about our daily affairs, we habitually flirt with death in ways that terrify strangers. Of this, the crowning example is the American automobile. It is an engine of destruction cunningly designed to repay with a ghastly death our slightest lapse of attention or error in judgment. We're more than half aware of its perils; yet we nevertheless love the automobile with a terrible passion. Even on a trivial errand the car gives us a chance to test ourselves against death and win.

For the same reason we are infatuated with such sickeningly dangerous sports as skiing (both on snow and water), skin-diving, hunting, surfing, and craziest of all, parachuting out of airplanes for fun.

Granted, a few of these games we Americans play against

death are still the property of a small minority. But what about the private game the commuter plays every time he bets his tired arteries he can win the sprint for his train? What about the pedestrian's own version of bullfighting, with oncoming cars as the *toros?* Or the acrobatics we perform on shaky ladders when we climb up to fix the roof? Unthinkingly—but with such zest!—everybody plays games like these. And far from being afraid to face death, Americans obviously love to have it near at hand. For without death, what would become of our feeling that life is a series of victories?

Our critics deplore that our leisure time is filled (so they insist) only with passive satisfactions. As "armchair Americans," we supposedly spend our free hours sitting in front of the television set and watching our favorite supercops kill off their enemies and our own. According to the usual overworked theory, this proves that only in fantasies of violence can Americans cope with death.

And yet, as in every other society, our heroes are only enlargements of ourselves, doing (though naturally on a heroic scale) what we ourselves do. Currently, for instance, Americans have one hero who is a bureaucrat. He has to show up at the office in the morning. He detests, but nevertheless completes, stacks of paper work. He submits to periodic job reviews. He's afraid of his boss, uneasy about his pension, and he often thinks half-heartedly about resigning. In private life, moreover, this hero is a finicky bachelor who fusses over his food and worries about his weight. He's also vain and a bit of a bore.

His name is James Bond.

Fascinated critics have said many different things about Ian Fleming's hero. But to us, one feature of Bond, at least in the books, should be especially significant: James is the servant of the ordinary. His adventures (and victories over death) start at the club, or on the golf course or the beach, or at a ski resort. Although he's a good shot, he hates guns. Indeed, the favorite weapons of this "pro killer" are those he carries around in a prosaic-looking briefcase or wears in his well-shined shoes. His most spectacularly destructive prop is a car. Like a good executive, Bond is at home everywhere. And like a good executive's hero, Bond never dies, but weaves, stumbles, and slips on his way through a world filled to overflowing with death. His reality is a souped-up version of our own.

In turn, our reality certainly cannot be said to shun or shrink away from death. On the contrary, in America death is as pervasive as patriotism. We react to death neither as cowards nor as children ignorant of the truth.

To account for those attitudes, we would have to dig into the American past. We'd have to see how different ideologies have been blended together—how, for instance, our traditional Protestantism has fused with our almost pagan belief in the inexhaustible bounty of the land we inhabit. Out of very ancient themes, Americans have put together a new, somehow mysterious, set of beliefs. The challenge is to recognize, without oversimplification, that the American way of death is in reality the American way of life.

At this point then, we can see that our dual themes, money and death, inevitably converge. And in a society such as ours, what other connection could we make than that money—our great life symbol—is used both symbolically and in fact to abolish death.

To support that hypothesis, an anthropologist would want to probe deeply into society; and that, of course, we can't do here. But even on the surface of society, the evidence is both plentiful and poignant. For instance, unlike medieval people, Americans don't leave money to pay for perpetual religious services for themselves after death. But our dead do bequeath money to endow universities for the young, hospitals to cure the sick, and research centers to win out over disease. The markers on our graves are growing smaller and less pretentious; and by the collective decision of all, our society, instead of commemorating the dead, taxes them for money to build schools, roads, and space rockets. At the very first glance, our society affords more examples than we can count that Americans think of money as the most important way of making death give place to life.

Pragmatically speaking, what exactly do these insights into American society tell us about life insurance, and how can we relate this seemingly remote theorizing to our own policies, our premiums, our beneficiaries? To begin with, life insurance is one of the best examples of our belief that money is life, and as life, helps us triumph over death. Because of that belief, we have made out of buying and selling life insurance a tremendous *symbolic* process—an almost sacramental one. We don't just own insurance, we *believe in* life insurance as a symbol of everything we do, think, and feel about defeating death.

Moreover, being Americans, we have carried this inner logic one step further by sponsoring and nurturing an *industry*—and not a religious, governmental, or charitable institution—to provide insurance. Just as insurance symbolizes our feelings about conquering death, so in turn does any industry, and especially this one, stand for the triumphant affirmation of our inexhaustible wealth, perpetual life, and ingenuity at outwitting death. Unlike ourselves, a great corporate entity is immortal.

This enshrinement of life insurance explains some of the industry's curious customs. For instance, to an insurance salesman, it's never "when you die," but "if you die"—as a matter of fact, agents are taught never to be so blunt and impolite as to mention death by name. "If, God forbid, anything should happen to you" is the stock way of suggesting that you are mortal. In similar fashion, life insurance advertising rarely mentions death. The favorite theme of the insurance ad is *life*. The industry talks constantly about the "living values" of insurance (the cash in the policy reserves that can be turned into retirement income). In the ads the illustrations almost always feature children.

"Hidden Attitudes Toward Life Insurance," the psychological research study mentioned in the last chapter, sums up perfectly this aspect of our insurance worship and suggests some reasons why the insurance trade should keep on selling life instead of life insurance.

> In the case of life insurance, the buyer knows logically that he is a mortal being, but there may be the wishful dream that, being prepared, he will escape . . . There is the possibility that magical thinking, so prevalent in unconscious attitudes toward other matters of deep fear, operates also toward life insurance. If it is indeed a magic talisman against the inevitable . . . the agent who stresses increasing life expectancy, new attitudes toward aging, and the importance of the *living* male in our society is often unknowingly, but effectively, selling this magic talisman.

According to one sophisticated salesman, the study is absolutely right. "The only reason people buy insurance is they think the policy is a magic charm guaranteeing them against death," says this psychiatrically oriented agent. "And the reason they *don't* buy is that they're afraid that the God of Death will know and point his finger at them."

We may or may not agree completely with this agent. But we do buy that $100,000,000,000 worth of insurance every year.

And during 1964 the industry paid out a total of $4,-

500,000,000 in death benefits, a sum equal to about one seventh of the total industry income for that year and to about one thirtieth of the life insurance industry's assets. Over 2,000,000 separate payments were made, reflecting the fact that most of the insurance owners who died carried more than one policy. (The industry does not reveal how many of its customers die during a given year.) The wide gap between payments and income means that life insurance in America is flourishing like the green bay tree. Small wonder that we regard the industry as one of our great vital symbols.

But no matter how effectively life insurance functions as a symbol, and despite the $4,500,000,000 pay-off, we also know that life insurance as a business is badly managed, inefficient, and above all terribly wasteful. We've seen that the men who run the industry operate by methods that are obsolete and that the quality of their performance is beyond our control. For this industry and these men to get away with so very much, doesn't there also have to be some other force at work? Our insurance policies cost us perhaps a third as much again as the mortality tables, investment yields, and expense ratios indicate they should. Most of us know or suspect that individually we pay a terrific price for life insurance—and we resent it. Yet as a society, we still go on taking out all that new insurance. Isn't it possible that, just as in the case of the funeral industry, we really *want* this product to be costlier and more complicated than life insurance needs to be?

To mention one more anthropological example, consider the Greek of ancient times who felt he must sacrifice to Zeus and knew that he should choose as his sacrificial beast not the skinniest but the fattest bull calf in the herd if he really wanted Zeus to befriend him. When it comes to buying life insurance, we seem to feel the same way: to count our pennies in this effort to defeat death is tempting the gods.

200

to blast us. Conversely, because we feel that the answer to death is an overflowing, superabundant life, we willingly pour into our insurance far more money, time, and energy than the final pay-off will ever justify. In short, for reasons that far transcend the practical, we ourselves share the blame for this institution's inadequacies and for the fact that our life insurance is more of a promise than a reality.

So what this society feels about life, death, and money does bear directly upon you and on what you can do about life insurance. Because Americans make a kind of cult out of insurance, you are caught in an inescapable web of traditions, customs, and attitudes. If you already own insurance, you may have bought it not out of necessity, but out of some vague feeling that everybody should have life insurance. You may be unaware that such social conditioning and not any actual need is making you buy; but the shrewd agent knows, and the industry knows, that rational planning has very little to do with your reaction to insurance. Such a situation may well frustrate and disgust you, for the American way of death may not be your own.

Having said that, there remains only one more thing for this book to do: show you how, as an individual, you can beat this system. We must still demonstrate that it's possible to use life insurance without being victimized by it and that you can, and probably should, come to terms with this peculiar institution.

> "There are no simple answers."
> —*the Lawyer, on estate planning*

10 . The Right *Way to Handle*
Life Insurance

BY NOW YOU MAY HEARTILY WISH that no such razor-sharp but double-edged product of human ingenuity as life insurance had ever been invented. Doubtless, you do wish there were some simpler and less painful way to solve your financial problems. Adding to your irritation may be your hunch that there *are* ways to beat this appalling system.

You are right. Given today's insurance industry, buying life insurance wisely is no easy proposition. But you certainly can handle your own insurance in ways that make it relatively cheap and easy to live with. Moreover, you can find the answers to your problems without becoming a life insurance expert (a self-defeating solution if ever there was one), and yet not be a patsy for the first agent who comes along. Though there are no easy solutions—no policies, plans, or programs that will once and for all take care of your needs— if you keep your wits about you, you can develop sound strategies for thinking about your requirements, for picking an agent who will *help* you, and for getting the maximum mileage out of the insurance you do buy.

In what follows, we'll be focusing mainly on such strategies, which means that we can't cover all the minute details of your policies or answer too many of the purely technical questions. (For instance, we can't debate whether you're better off using a large company or a small one, a stock company or a mutual.) On the other hand, if you follow the signposts and suggestions in this chapter, they will lead you straight to specialists who can and will educate you in the nuances that are omitted here.

In order to deal shrewdly with life insurance, you must first of all recognize and then never forget that your own needs are as unique as you are. Never mind what your neighbor does (or thinks or says he does). Disregard those nonsensical rules of thumb that say you need enough insurance to replace five years' worth of income or that you should budget 5 per cent of your income for insurance. (Why? Why not six years' worth or 6 per cent of income? Why not three years' worth or 4 per cent?) What you yourself eventually do about life insurance depends upon only one thing: *what you yourself think and feel about life, death, and money.* Nobody—no expert, no salesman, no outside party—can formulate for you the answers to these most personal inner questions.

You may not believe in life insurance at all. You may be thoroughly and forgivably disenchanted with the insurance to which you've been exposed or feel that there are better ways than life insurance to accomplish your own goals. You may be single, without dependents. Finally, you may believe (as surprisingly many people believe, whether or not they admit it) that death should release the individual from any obligation to the living.

At the other end of the spectrum, however, there are those who feel not an obligation but a loving concern to provide generously for their dependents. Some people feel that present sacrifice is called for in order to make such ample provision. Thus, you may actually take pride in owning as much life insurance as you can possibly afford to carry.

Most of us fall somewhere between these two extremes, though probably few of us know just where we do stand on the subject of what should happen when (not if) we die. This fuzzy-mindedness is precisely what makes us so vulnerable to the threats and blandishments of the Man with a Plan. The beginning of wisdom about life insurance consists, not of a short course in life insurance itself, but of a certain amount of meditation on the consequences of dying. Pick your own time and place, but do a bit of brooding. The fruits of your contemplation may surprise you very much.

You may realize, for example, that you've never really discussed with your wife this subject of death. Therefore, you are quite uncertain of exactly how she would feel if you were to wrap your car around a tree or to contract a fatal disease. Having decided to broach such a possibility to her, you may be moved, shocked, or astonished to learn what her attitudes really are. Similarly, if your children are old enough to understand something of death, their feelings, too, may take you by surprise.

To die without knowing that some things were taken care of and that certain events were definitely going to happen would probably frustrate you. (According to surveys sponsored by the airlines, premature death actually *embarrasses* us more than anything else.) Precisely what those things and events are depends in turn on who you are, what you do, and what you want—out of life, not death. Thus, if you are wealthy, your chief concern may be that your fortune is conveyed safely to whomever you choose to enrich by your death. This may mean that you have or need the advice of many specialists—lawyers, accountants, and tax and other financial advisors.

But even if you aren't wealthy, your final concerns about death and money still depend on your age, family status, income, and place in the social order. Therefore, your next step is to think about money in terms of what, if anything, you consider most important for your survivors. For instance, you may urgently feel that whether or not you're alive to foot the bills, your children should be financially able to go to college and perhaps even to graduate or professional school as well. Yet in thinking about college, be careful neither to oversimplify nor to overcomplicate your problem. You may feel that college is more important for your sons than for your daughters. You may secretly suspect that your kids are bright enough to win scholarships or that if they want higher education, they'll somehow find ways to get it. If so, you may worry more about there being enough money to feed, clothe, and shelter your kids until they are old enough to take care of themselves. Or your children may already be of age, and your main concern is to leave enough money to provide for your spouse. Most of us have no trouble at all piling up reasons to die rich rather than poor.

Let's assume that you've already done a certain amount of thinking. No doubt, you have decided that you can't possibly leave enough money to pay all your debts (including your mortgage), to support your family in the style to which you have accustomed them, to finance college education all around, and to take care of your widow in her old age. To fulfill a complete list of such post-mortem "obligations," you think ruefully, I'd have to be a millionaire.

Exactly.

As remarkable as our society is, it still offers only partial solutions to the economic problems that death creates. Once you accept this fact, you can begin to appraise those partial solutions realistically. You are now, in fact, just starting to do the job that *includes* dealing with life insurance. Your homework must also take into account such matters as the property you own, your will, and your Social Security. You must also be aware of the problems and possibilities that specialists lump together under the category of "estate planning."

What's in Your Estate?

Your estate is simply the property—including money—you own when you die. Of course, this seemingly straightforward definition has many ramifications. Property can be anything, from intangibles like copyrights or royalties to objects as solid as twenty-four-carat-gold jewelry. You may own real property (for instance, a house), personal property (your car), or like most people, both. Regardless of what you own, however, you're almost sure to have an estate, and the simplest way to determine what it contains is to make an inventory of all your property. If you don't think you own much property, take a notebook and a walk around the house and yard. The sum total of your material possessions (including such random items as your electric lawn mower and the half-dozen bottles of liquor in your pantry) may startle you.

Having made that physical inventory, you can next settle down to figure just what portion of your property is really yours; i.e., legally belongs to you. If you're a fairly substantial citizen, you may not be able to do this all by yourself—and now would be a good time to call in a lawyer and an accountant. Even if you think that in your own modest case, this question of ownership is perfectly straightforward, be very careful. For instance, in whose name is the deed to your house? If the house is in your name, you actually own it, and the value of the house is therefore part of *your* estate. But if you and your wife own the house together, as is very often the case, don't think that only half of its value could wind up in your estate. On the contrary, most of the time the full value will be included in the estate of *whichever* spouse dies first. This fact could have decidedly unpleasant legal and tax consequences, especially if you yourself died suddenly.

Similarly, fine details of law may govern the ownership of your other property to such an extent that to be on the safe side, you should discuss this whole matter with your lawyer. If you don't have a lawyer, get one. In any case, you'll need a lawyer for the next step, drawing your will.

YOUR WILL

There is no excuse for not having a will. If you've struggled hard to accumulate property, it's madness not to take so reasonable a precaution about what happens to your property when you die. Otherwise, you leave the question of who gets what to the dubious wisdom of your state legislature and the local courts, which create and enforce the so-called "intestate laws." As your lawyer will tell you, dying intestate (without a will) is almost worse than dying broke, for your survivors, instead of inheriting property, will inherit a mess. To avoid such a situation usually takes no more than a couple of visits to your lawyer. So make the arrangements. His advice will save you and your heirs a great deal more money than the price of his fee.

Here again, this may be saying the obvious. You may not only take for granted the need to have a will, but also have ideas about trusts and other special legal instruments. Nevertheless, even successful men forget that their plans for disposing of their estate can quickly become outdated. The faster you climb the ladder, the more often you may need to review and revise your will and other estate arrangements. So if you've already made one will, ask yourself how recent it is and be prepared to give your lawyer a call anyway.

That part of your estate which is transferred to your heirs by will is called your "probate estate." Because you normally name a beneficiary to get the proceeds of your life insurance policies, life insurance money is not governed by your will and is thus not usually part of your probate estate. This may be why many men believe that as far as the estate is concerned, life insurance doesn't count. But unless you have made certain specific changes in your policies, your insurance is included in your general (or "gross") estate. As in the case of your home, this unexpected inclusion of a large-sized asset may have undesirable tax consequences. Your lawyer will help you decide the best way to handle such a possible problem. See him and take his advice.

Finally, you may feel that your estate is too small to bother with, that planning the disposition of such a sparse inheritance is hardly worth the time and effort. Every reputable lawyer, every respectable estate-planning specialist, and every text on the subject will tell you that you are making a disastrous mistake. Thus, you may own what most men own: a house with a mortgage, a car with the payments not yet completed, a few hundred dollars in the checking account, a thousand or so in savings, some U.S. Bonds, perhaps a few shares of stock, and $20,000 worth of life insurance. Your total estate is worth perhaps $60,000, and by the time you subtract the outstanding mortgage and car loans, you are leaving your family something like half that amount. On that kind of money, your family won't be living in luxury for very long. With Social Security, however, there may be enough to get by on; and properly handled, a few thousand extra dollars can make a great deal of difference. The only way to make sure that court costs, unnecessary legal fees, and the like don't eat up at least that much money is to leave a proper will, together with a letter of instruction to your executor (the person who handles your estate). Your plans need not be complicated; your will may be only one page long. But, without both, you're throwing away money that would go to your heirs.

SOCIAL SECURITY

Because you don't "own" the benefits, the money payable to your surviving family under Social Security isn't actually part of your estate. But such "survivorship benefits" under federal Social Security may add up to an astonishingly large chunk of cash, assuming that you die leaving children who are minors. Under the present Social Security provisions, for instance, a man who dies leaving children aged four and two "bequeaths" (if he's fully covered) $254 a month to his youngsters until the four-year-old reaches age eighteen. This monthly income then drops to $174 until the younger child also reaches eighteen. After that, payments stop. To equal this cash pay-out under Social Security, the father would have to leave his children $38,981. So Social Security obviously makes a great deal of difference.

However, trying to explain Social Security is just like trying to explain the New York City subway system. Everything depends on where you are now and where you're going. If you feel that you should find out more about Social Security, your bank, to name one place that has access to the information, is a good center of inquiry. And for specific information about your own Social Security account, you can write (on special forms obtainable at your local post office) to the following address: Social Security Administration, 6401 Security Boulevard, Baltimore, Maryland.

GIFTS AND INHERITANCES

In thinking about your own estate, you'd definitely be wise to consider what someone else may be planning to give or bequeath to you and your family. Your plans, after all, could be sharply altered by the plans of others, or their intentions nullified by what you yourself do. To give one example, if you expect to inherit a sizable sum—$50,000 or more, let's say—your own life insurance should be arranged very differently from what might otherwise be most reasonable. You should buy term insurance that would cover your needs until the time when you expected to receive the inheritance. Then you should probably buy permanent insurance, enough so that your own newly enlarged estate would contain liquid cash for death-tax purposes. The difference can save you quite a lot of premium money and also preserve the inheritance intact for your survivors if you die before spending it.

In dealing with possible gifts and bequests, your main problem is that the donor will probably prefer to be silent —too silent—on the subject. Thus, the gap between the generations is never wider than when money is involved. Even though a minimum of information can sometimes save both old and young much money (in taxes and insurance premiums), children are embarrassed, ashamed, and unwilling to question their parents; and parents are reluctant to confide in their children. But if you can find a way to communicate with your potential benefactors, try to get a fairly precise idea of where you stand so that you'll be able to make the best arrangements.

LIFE INSURANCE

Having gone over these preliminaries, and having read this book, your ideas about life insurance should certainly be in much sharper focus. As you now know, life insurance is not packaged immortality. You don't automatically bless your house by owning a couple of policies. Nor by casually assuming that the policies you do own contain all the answers, do you even begin to solve the economic problems raised by death. Yet among all the other partial solutions to those problems, life insurance can and must play an important role. For most of us, life insurance is the only way we can leave an estate of respectable size. Of those who are concerned about death and money, only a tiny percentage can afford to do entirely without life insurance. Today even the very rich don't scorn insurance.

The wealthy insurance buyer attracts expert, unbiased advice because he believes in paying for it. Only if by chance we encounter a knowledgeable, helpful, low-pressure insurance man do the rest of us get such advice. And since this almost never happens, let's come to grips with the insurance agent you do get and discover how to select, deal with, outwit, and profit by transactions with your own insurance man —and, on occasion, to ignore him.

PICKING A GOOD LIFE INSURANCE AGENT

A "good" agent really means someone who is qualified in two ways—as a businessman and as a person. Only you can judge the sort of individual who meets your own personal standards. But even though this makes the job of selecting an agent harder, you should *never* ignore your own feelings about the man who may someday play a key role in your family's life. "He's a good insurance man, but I just don't *like* the so-and-so" is the habitual gripe of millions of insurance buyers. With agents in such long supply, why on earth put up with one whose personality annoys you? Because life insurance is so intimate and private a business, you should first of all want your agent to have the right personal touch ("a combination of delicacy, warmth, and authority," one astute agent put it). So ask yourself about your present agent: Do I like him? Within the limits of his job as a salesman, can I trust him? Only if your man does measure up to what you want personally should you even bother about his insurance qualifications.

This definitely means that you should pick your agent rather than being picked by him. If you happen to know a number of insurance men, you've got a ready-made list from which to make your selection. If none of your acquaintances seems like an ideal choice, however, go elsewhere.

You owe nobody, not even your brother, your life insurance business. If your brother's a great guy who happens also to be a fine insurance man, that's another story. But if your brother or a cousin or an old chum has "just gone into the business" and is soliciting you to buy, for heaven's sake put him off. By "taking his policy," you're not doing him any favor, but you may be doing both him and your family a profound disservice. To become successful in his trade, a new insurance man must first of all learn to operate among strangers. And if he is to help you and yours, any insurance man must be reasonably successful. So the real favor you do your relative is to say, "Larry, you're brand-new at life insurance. My own insurance is in very good hands at the moment"—say this even if it's not true—"and I won't consider making any change. So let's not embarrass each other. If there's any way I can help, other than by buying insurance from you . . ." There are so many "orphans" (policy owners who have no agent) and so many new customers that you're not depriving Larry of anything. But if you do buy insurance from him, you almost certainly are depriving yourself of a good insurance man.

While we're on the subject, you might also find it useful to know how to turn down requests for insurance interviews. Some people seem to be natural targets for solicitations, either in person or over the telephone, while others don't hear from eager salesmen for months on end. But if you do get an annoying number of telephone calls, the best response is to wait until he has introduced himself and then say politely but firmly, "No. Thank you for calling." (If you're particularly soft-hearted, you can add some such phrase as "I realize you have a great many calls to make." You may then either wait for his farewell—or hang up. To a hard-working telephone solicitor, such abruptness won't seem rude. On the contrary, your terse refusal frees him to move on to the next name on his list; and the truly proficient telephone artist wants to converse with people who will see him, not argue with people who won't.

The same technique can be applied to the increasingly rare occasions when an insurance man comes unbidden to your door. Take a leaf from his book, bare *your* teeth in a big smile, and say, "No. But thank you for stopping by." Before closing the door, step back and wait for him to turn away. You thus avoid the mutual embarrassment of slamming the door in his face.

In brushing off solicitations, always remember that the important word is "No"—not "Well, I don't need any" or "Gee, I'm awfully sorry, but"—just "No." Today's solicitors *will* take "No" for an answer. Furthermore, if you teach your wife the techniques of saying "No" firmly, you may be able to avoid those little family scenes that arise when she tells you after dinner that a nice insurance man came by that afternoon and made an appointment to see you the same evening.

Avoiding solicitors is half the battle. The other half is selecting a good permanent agent. Perhaps the best way to treat the matter is to think of your own insurance as a job, to be handled by the best-qualified applicant you can find. Thus, having made that short list of the insurance men you know (and if necessary getting your local banker or your lawyer to add some names), you then actually *interview* each man on the list. When you call, tell each agent that you have certain insurance problems and that you'd like to set up an appointment to discuss them. Once the shock has worn off, the various salesmen will gladly agree to see you at your convenience.

The best place to interview your candidates is an office, preferably your own (if it's private). Next best is some neutral private location, such as a club, a restaurant, or other outside meeting spot. *The last place you'll want to use for these interviews is your own home.* As we've seen, this is the one locale the agent has been trained to exploit. Since the purpose of this interviewing scheme is for *you* to control these first encounters, conduct your interviews where you can most easily stay in command of the situation.

GETTING THE JUMP ON THE AGENT

You aren't hiring an executive to take command of your million-dollar company. Nevertheless, you are choosing someone to look after your interests and to advise you about one of the largest personal expenditures you're likely to make during your lifetime. That's why this interview approach (which takes almost longer to describe than to carry out) makes so much sense. If you yourself are a top executive, you doubtless understand all the little tricks that keep you on top in an interview. But if you're not accustomed to directing men's attention to what you want to discuss, interviewing may leave you at something of a loss. Therefore, the following may prove helpful.

As each of your candidates shows up for his appointment, get the necessary formalities over promptly. Then say to the agent, "I've asked you here to give me your ideas about my life insurance. But before we begin, do you mind if *I* first ask *you* a couple of questions?"

Without being an insurance man yourself, you naturally won't be able to quiz your candidate searchingly on the innermost details of his business qualifications. But here are three key questions that will tell you, with surprising predictability, just how responsible an agent you are talking to:

(1) How long have you been in the life insurance business?
(2) What's the best policy your company has to offer?
(3) How much insurance would you say I ought to own?

All three questions are polite and good-humored—but revealing. You won't offend any agent by asking them. And yet, from the replies they give, you can learn a great deal— much more than they will even suspect—about your candidates.

Thus, if one of them answers Question 1 by telling you that he's been in the life insurance business three years or less, you know right away (even if *he* doesn't) that his chances of staying in the business are slender. So unless you have some special reason for knowing that he's going to stick, get rid of him. Don't waste time on lengthy explanations; just rise, offer him your hand, and say, "I'm sorry. I definitely have in mind someone with a great deal more experience." Thank him for coming in—and show him out.

Once again, you have no reason to get involved with a beginner. Such an involvement only means that because you served as a guinea pig for some raw insurance recruit, your family may have to suffer. Under normal circumstances, five years is the *minimum* length of experience you should accept as enough. Above all, if for any reason you suspect the agent is lying about his experience, throw him out in a hurry.

If the candidate satisfies you about his experience, go on to Questions 2 and 3. Depending upon whether the man you are seeing happens to be a good salesman, a conscientious insurance man, or both, his answers will vary. Don't worry. More important than what the candidate says is the way he says it. So be listening for all those undertones—the hint of shrillness, the exhortation, the overly glib or slick answer—that this book has taught you to expect. Listen, too, for defensiveness and signs of irritation. And *if the agent gives you precise answers,* be on your guard. For instance, if he replies to Question 2 by saying, "Well, our best policy is the Executive Provider Three-Year Modified Special," then you know that this agent thinks in terms of policies and very likely in terms of gimmicked-up insurance as well. (We'll get to some of the gimmicks a little later.) Remember that you can buy a policy from a machine at the airport. You're not looking for a policy, but for an intangible and complex service.

Especially beware of the agent who tells you that his company's plans are the best plans. He won't know. Indeed, how could he? Five hundred companies, all offering scores of different insurance contracts, may do business in your state.

Any agent who expects you to believe that he has made, or is even qualified to make, all the necessary comparisons is a liar.

A sensible answer to Question 2 is, "Mr. Customer, there isn't any best company or policy. We're all pretty much alike. There is only sound insurance and unsound insurance, and what may be valid for you may not be at all good for your neighbor. So to tell you the truth, I can't answer that question." The agent who will level with you on Question 2 is a fair bet to be honest about all your other questions and your needs.

Such an agent might answer Question 3 by telling you that until he knows certain basic facts about you, he can't possibly make any recommendations about the proper amount of insurance for you to own. He *may* even add that your own feelings about insurance are what count and that his job is to help you set your ideas in order. If he's what the ads call "a real pro," he'll then sit back and wait for you to make the next move. In a moment we'll see what that move should be.

But first let's take time to mention that neither the agent's skill nor the company's reputation is subject to accurate measurement. Thus, you must be especially wary of any claims a given candidate makes about himself. For example, in 999 cases out of 1,000, the insurance man whose business card reads "Insurance Consultant" is no more a consultant than is your local TV repairman an "Electronics Consultant." (The acid test that separates the phony from the genuine insurance consultant is simple: the true consultant *never* sells insurance; he works only on a fee basis. The faker only pretends to work for a fee. If you buy insurance from him, you get your fee back.)

At another extreme, the grandly named American College

of Life Underwriters has long sponsored an elaborate program of agent education—a five-part course covering insurance, law, economics, finance, and something called the Practice of Life Underwriting (which is only a fancy term for salesmanship). Completion of this program qualifies the agent for the Chartered Life Underwriter (or C.L.U.) degree; he gets a diploma and a nice gold key to wear on his necktie. Backed by heavy industry subsidies, the American College is earnestly trying to elevate the C.L.U. designee to "professional" status, like that of the accountant who's a C.P.A.

Alas, the C.L.U. program is tainted, to say the least, with that gilt-edged but heavy-handed salesmanship we just mentioned. While publicly endorsing the "professional" aims and ideals of the college, life insurance companies privately subvert the program by helping their agents become C.L.U.'s —in order to sell more insurance. Agents are urged to take three, four, or five parts of the course in one year in hopes that even if they can't study all the material, they'll pass an extra exam. Company-run cram courses are commonplace. Therefore, most aspirants are interested in grabbing the designation only for prestige, and they joke about not wanting or needing to master the rather simple study guides and texts. This cynicism about education means that you yourself cannot rely on C.L.U. designees to be what they claim to be. Rather, because a little superficial knowledge is a dangerous thing, you are almost better off with a reasonably practiced, sympathetic non-C.L.U. (who at least knows his own limitations) than with one of these self-styled "professionals."

All things considered, you do best to rely on your own judgment about your own candidates. If you go about the search for a good agent with the determination to screen each candidate carefully, your instincts will tell you when you find the right man. Your best protection is to relax and take your time. Eventually you will find an agent who does measure up, and you'll be a lot happier for having taken the trouble to choose wisely.

But even when you do feel that you've found the right man for your insurance job, don't allow him to turn your screening interview into a sales interview. Keep control of the situation by making a definite future appointment with your new agent—to discuss insurance. If he's the man you're looking for, he'll understand exactly what you're doing and why and he'll respect you for your good judgment.

Dealing with the Agent

Your next appointment with the agent should be at home. This time, however, you've met your man and you know what to expect, so there's no chance of being caught off balance by his hearthside sales pitch. Furthermore, at this point you will want your wife to meet the agent and to join in the discussion. You will also want the agent to meet your wife.

You want definite information—facts, figures, and ideas —upon which to base decisions about life insurance. You know, however, that the agent will primarily want you to *buy* the insurance. Thus, you must let your agent know that as far as you're concerned, he's an adviser, a source of essential information, and an ally. Tell him that you've made up your mind to consider his suggestions and trust his judgment, that you're not "shopping around" or calling up his competitors.

But make it clear that you cannot either be pushed or cajoled into a quick purchase.

220·

The conscientious agent will be flattered by your attitude and will also realize that to get and keep your account, he'll have to give you better-than-average service. Even though he's not a professional, by treating him as if he were, you almost force him to act like one—and this in turn takes the pressure off *you*.

This interview should last no longer than an hour. You can speed things along by having right at hand all the various documents you think you might need: your present policies, your group-insurance certificates, if any, and the like. If you think other papers would be useful—your mortgage or your will, for instance—have them available also. And you might jot down, too, any questions about your present insurance that you'd like to have answered right away. Indeed, the most important ground rule for dealing with the agent is to ask questions—even those that seem to you embarrassingly simple—until you're absolutely certain you understand what the agent is driving at. Insurance is complicated enough that unless you're used to reasoning in terms of its concepts, you can easily *think* you know more than you do know. Therefore, you're better off assuming you're ignorant. A good agent will patiently untangle any bothersome problem or question.

If the agent sees a high pile of policy booklets and other documents at your elbow, he may suggest drawing up a schedule or inventory of your present insurance. (If you happen to be dealing with an experienced estate-planning specialist, he'll insist on making a record of your non-insurance holdings as well.) That's fine, but have the agent give you a receipt for any policies or papers he takes away with him; and also set a deadline by which your policies must be returned. A capable insurance agent can make a survey of your existing policies almost while you're sitting there. There's no reason to let him procrastinate, keeping your policies on his desk for weeks (or months) until he gets around to analyzing them.

By the time this interview is over, you and the agent should have established some kind of rapport. By listening to your questions and by asking questions of his own, he will have found out what possible needs and problems are preoccupying you. And if he thinks you need more insurance (what agent doesn't?), he'll tell you so.

This leaves several possibilities open. If you agree that you do have a need, ask him to prepare a signed proposal of his suggestions, to mail it to you, and then to revisit you for further discussion. (Make a definite appointment now for that next visit. Otherwise, the agent may figure you're just trying to get rid of him.)

If you feel that you don't happen to need life insurance right now, this is the time to say so—and this is the time to offer the agent a flat fee for analyzing your present insurance. The fee doesn't have to be a large one. Unless you've got really complicated problems, $25 will pay for his time and effort. And you have no idea what your offer will mean to the agent! By making him draw up your "program" for free and then turning him down, you'd be exploiting him rather meanly. Instead, you're buying very reasonably the objective advice you need. The grateful agent will be your friend for life; and what's more important, your modest investment will buy you a great deal of valuable information.

However, if you're undecided about needing life insurance, make that clear at the end of this initial interview. If your agent truly understands what you expect of him, he'll certainly try to sell you on that next interview, but his selling will be relaxed and low-pressure.

Between Interviews

While your agent is busy preparing his inventory of your present insurance and his proposal of what he thinks you should buy, you must give the matter some thought yourself. If you've already offered your man a fee for a service job, you have little to ponder until he returns with his policies. But if you think you should buy more insurance or even if you're still undecided, you should prepare for the agent's return by figuring out what amount of money you *could* scrape together in order to buy additional insurance. No matter what your agent proposes, no matter how persuasively he tries to sell you what he thinks is right, your insurance buying must always be based on what you can afford. If you figure out in advance what that sum might be, you'll be much better off. If you let the agent help you, the way Henry Cox "helped" in Chapter 1, you'll be sorry! So never mind the amount or kind of insurance the agent will ask you to buy. You must decide on the price and then let him tailor his proposal accordingly.

Obviously, if he's mailed you a proposal that dovetails exactly with what you want to spend, everything is much simpler. But if he feels you need more insurance than you think you can afford, the two of you must necessarily compromise. Be prepared to do so. Assuming that his suggestions make good sense, you're better off buying some insurance than none at all.

The Next Interview

If you have already agreed with your agent on a fee-paid service interview, you have no problem beyond that of making sure you understand what your agent tells you. So review his report with him, pay him his fee, and let him go. If he suggests having changes made, sign his prepared statement authorizing him to act as your agent and have him go ahead. Conversely, if you definitely plan to buy, you and the agent should decide what, if any, modifications in his proposal are necessary. Then you can proceed with the company's application, medical exam, and so on. (Very shortly, we'll come back to focus on this actual buying process.) But if you are uncertain about whether or not you *should* buy insurance, you run into a tricky problem, for no matter how sincere he may be, your agent *will* try to sell you—and in trying, only confuse you all the more.

There's no cut-and-dried answer to this problem. What you finally do will depend in part on how flexible your own attitudes are and also on whether or not your agent does persuade you. However, so that you will be somewhat prepared, we can look into some of the more common methods of persuasion.

For instance, if you're thirty-five and you now carry $50,000 worth of life insurance, the agent can make your coverage look shamefully inadequate. He can show you that $5,000 of your insurance money would be immediately dissipated in "final expenses"—medical and funeral bills, legal fees, taxes, and the like—after you died. He can demonstrate that the remaining $45,000 is worth only about $5,000 a year for ten years following your death. (The interest earned while the insurance company slowly pays out the principal is worth an extra $5,000.) In short, for someone of your means, $50,000 worth of insurance is pretty paltry protection. Don't you want your children to go to college? Don't you want your widow to spend her declining years in *dignity?* Well, in order to solve such problems, $50,000 just isn't enough, Mr. Customer, is it?

That in essence is the so-called "programming approach" to dramatizing your insurance needs.

To avoid being hypnotized by the seemingly irrefutable logic of that approach, your best defense is to remember that *nobody can afford enough insurance to replace more than a small fraction of his own earning power.* Thus, suppose that at thirty-five you're earning $15,000 a year. If you did die tomorrow (and the odds against your dying are 500 to one), your demise would presumably deprive your family of at least thirty years' worth of income. Even if you don't figure in bonuses or raises, that loss would amount to a cool $450,000 (your salary multiplied by the number of years left until retirement). To carry that much life insurance would bankrupt you. At your age, $450,000 of permanent insurance costs about $10,000 a year. (The same amount of term insurance to age sixty-five costs more than $7,000 yearly.) Thus, such "total insurance" would soak up half to two thirds of your gross income. Think how silly you'd feel if you actually spent all that money—and then didn't die before retirement.

Now, even the hungriest agent won't push the programming approach to such ridiculous extremes. Rather, he will use it to make you think big, and perhaps buy $50,000 rather than the piddling $5,000 you might otherwise have bought. So when the agent starts blowing up this immense balloon, be prepared to pop it from within.

Realizing that insurance can never be more than a partial solution to the economic disaster of untimely death, you should find that the "single need" (or "package") approach is better suited to your requirements. As the name suggests, this approach lets the agent help you draw a line around some basic needs—education funds, mortgage-cancellation money, income to supplement Social Security—that insurance is well suited to solve. The agent then assists you in deciding what priority you give your needs; for example, whether you care more about college for your children or about having your mortgage paid off. Only after you assign definite priorities does the agent work out with you what additional insurance you should buy.

This approach, too, is designed to persuade as well as inform you. But it has the advantage of making you think about insurance in relatively precise terms. You *can* match insurance to the size of your mortgage or the price of a college education. As a result, you may recognize that you have insurance needs you weren't aware of. Don't give your agent the chance to wing off into the blue on a programming approach. Insist instead that he take up your needs one at a time, and make him keep his discussion both simple and specific.

By the time he has finished, you should have an excellent idea of whether or not you do need more insurance; and you already know, of course, how much more you could budget to pay for it. Once again, get the jump on the agent. Tell him that you like the idea of insurance for college (or whatever) and that you can afford right now to spend $5 more a week for a policy. "What will that buy me?" Naturally, an insurance man would much rather sell something than nothing. So he'll be quick with suggestions for fitting his own recommendations into your budget. He himself will know as well as you do that to overstrain you financially is foolish. Why should he kill the goose that lays even modest golden eggs? Besides, if you can't afford it, you'll simply drop the policy, and the lapse will be a black mark on his record.

How to Buy Insurance

The really good agent wants you to mull over his facts, figures, and ideas at leisure. So while you ruminate, he'll sit quietly, speaking only in response to your questions. Nevertheless, you may decide to schedule still another interview before letting your agent know your decision. As a kindness to him, make that appointment definite, too. Don't leave things on an "I'll call *you*" basis. If and when you do decide to take out the additional insurance, the following procedure makes sense and saves both of you time and trouble.

(1) Complete the application.
(2) On the spot, write your check for as much of the yearly premium as you can afford to pay (the company tacks on a hefty service charge for semiannual, quarterly, or monthly payments).
(3) Arrange as soon as possible to be examined by the company doctor.

If you're sure that you need and want this insurance, you have everything to gain by speedy action, since presumably you need the insurance *now* and you may be losing something if you delay. As your agent will tell you, "You'll never be healthier or younger than you are today." So once having decided to buy, why stall around?

Above all, tell the agent the truth about your past personal and medical history, about your employment and financial record, about everything. If you have any impairment that might make the Underwriting Department nervous, be open about it. Concealment might cost you extra, where frankness might get you a standard-rate policy. To hide something from the agent or the doctor and then to get indignant about being rated up is silly and a waste of time. If you're doubtful about your health status, have the agent submit you to Underwriting as a nameless hypothetical applicant. That way, a rating or declination won't crop up on your Medical Information Bureau record and destroy any future chance of getting standard (or any other) insurance. But when he says that a man in only fair health needs whatever life insurance

he can get, your agent may be right. So put aside your ego
and be prepared to pay extra for your policy.

Two weeks after you apply for the insurance, the policy
should be in your hands. Don't let the agent mail you the
contract. Insist that he deliver it in person and verify with
him that the policy's details are exactly what you understood they would be. If your automobile dealer delivered a
new car that was different from what the car salesman had
promised, you'd go storming down to the showroom to set
things straight. If anything, you should exercise even more
care about your life insurance. It's a lot more expensive than
any car you're likely to buy.

How to Say "No"

Your agent's done a lot of work. He's waded through your
existing policies and inventoried them for you. He's answered
endless questions and made certain very sensible suggestions
about life insurance—including a reasonable recommen-
dation that you buy more. You admire his style and respect
his *expertise*.

Nevertheless, you should be the one to decide, if necessary,
that you just don't want more life insurance. Later on you
may feel differently. But at the moment other things are
more important. And so you must say "No" to your agent.

Say "no"—not "Maybe" or "Give me a few weeks on
this." If he's done a really fine job of explaining and recom-
mending, tell him how grateful you are and offer him the
same modest fee we considered earlier. He'll be flattered and
grateful in return, and he may even refuse your money. If
you plan to buy from him later on, tell him that he's gained
a future customer and have him keep your name on his call-
back list. Take him to lunch, and you pick up the tab. But
above all, when you do turn him down, watch your agent's re-

action. If he accepts your decision without getting aggravated or petulant and without making any last-ditch effort to change your mind, you may well have found a man to take care of your life insurance permanently. Hang on to the relationship, for as you know, such agents aren't easy to find.

What Else Is in Those Policies?

Throughout this book we've been seeing that life insurance in general is overpriced. However, no life insurance policy is "good" simply because it seems cheap or "bad" just because it appears expensive. Given the limitations of all life insurance, each form of policy is a tool with certain special uses. Thus, it's utterly senseless to favor one form arbitrarily over another. Picking out the particular form (or combination of forms) that's best suited to your needs is your agent's task. And if you take the trouble to find a capable insurance man, his good offices should automatically solve this problem.

But no matter what kind of insurance you happen to own, you should be aware that certain extra features may be making your policies even more expensive than you had bargained for. On the other hand, you may be pleased to find that your policies also contain certain extras that actually make your insurance more valuable. So while we needn't go into copious detail, let's at least examine a few of these extras to see which of them are merely tail fins and which do in fact serve a functional purpose.

Waiver of Premium and Double Indemnity

Most agents give their customers no choice about whether or not to buy these two extras. The agent simply includes them, adding their cost into the total premium. As you may already know, "waiver of premium" is a kind of disability benefit attachable to life insurance. From company to company, details vary, but the usual waiver-of-premium arrangement is as follows. If you become disabled (and thereby suffer the loss of earning ability) while you own the policy, the insurance company will begin to pick up the tab for your policy after an initial six-month waiting period. The company will then return to you any premium you paid during that initial six months. For as long as your disability lasts, the company will keep on paying the premiums. But when you recover, you owe nothing.

Waiver of premium obviously makes good sense. Even though the price of this extra benefit increases your insurance cost by 2.5 to 5 per cent, the threat of long-term disability is serious enough to justify such an expense. So have your agent add waiver of premium to your policies.

However, "double indemnity" (or more accurately, "accidental-death benefit") is a very different kettle of fish. For still another 4 per cent of your premium, this extra provides that double the policy's face amount will be paid if you die by accident. (Many companies now sweeten their accidental-death benefit by paying *triple* the face amount if you die by accident as "a fare-paying passenger on a common carrier"; i.e., a plane, train, bus, etc.)

But why should accidental death be worth twice or three times as much to your survivors as death *not* by accident? Either way, you're just as dead. If your present insurance is adequate, you don't need to provide the extra insurance. And if your present insurance is less than sufficient, then buying a form of insurance that covers you only a small part of the time is no sort of solution. In short, double indemnity is strictly a gamble—that you'll be lucky enough to die in an accident and thereby leave your family a windfall. By now you should know that unless they hold all the cards, life insurance companies don't gamble. Therefore, and especially if you don't travel a great deal, you are better off not carrying double indemnity.

Other Tail Fins

In addition to the usual waiver of premium, a very few companies still offer "disability income benefits" of $10 or $20 a month for every $1,000 worth of insurance. If some of your old policies contain such provision, you're lucky. During the 1920's many companies granted the income benefit as a merchandising gimmick and charged a very modest price. Today, however, disability-income insurance is much costlier across the board. To offer an income as part of waiver of premium, companies now charge you a 6 or 7 per cent surcharge in addition to the waiver-of-premium charge. Forget it. (You should be buying separate disability-income insurance anyway).

For another 10 per cent or thereabouts, you can also add to your policy what most companies call a "guaranteed insurability rider," a clause that permits you (at specified future dates) to buy additional policies at standard rates, regardless of the state of your health. This, too, is a merchandising gimmick. It's the company's attempt to tie up your future insurance purchases.

There's nothing really wrong with any of these tail-fin options. But given half a chance, an agent will chrome-plate your basic policy with them. Though the benefits remain pretty much unchanged, the cost of the policy (and the agent's commission) will creep higher. If you want to keep your insurance outlay down, tell your agent to forget about all the options except waiver of premium. If you should later change your mind about some or all of these extras, you could easily have them added.

The Valuable Options

On the advantageous side, one of the smartest ways to buy insurance for some purposes is to add one or more optional term-insurance riders to your basic permanent policy. If you decide, for instance, to take out insurance that would provide money to pay off a mortgage, you can match the mortgage with term insurance that decreases as you pay off more and more of the mortgage debt. The insurance can be carried as a rider (or supplement) to an existing policy, usually at less cost than for a separate contract. Rather secretively, the major companies are trying to make such combination policies attractive—like those tools that have a variety of blades you can fit into a single handle. Most agents detest this company effort. The agent makes more money selling separate policies. But you should check with your agent about such multipurpose combinations.

Settlement Options

As you probably know, instead of leaving your life insurance dollars to be paid out in one lump sum, you can arrange other systems of payment. In fact, your policy's "settlement options" (as "explained" in those complicated tables you find somewhere in the policy itself) make possible almost any scheme of payment you or your beneficiaries desire. For instance, you can have the company pay your family a steady income every month for a given number of years. You can provide for some of your insurance proceeds to be paid out at once, while a balance remains on deposit at interest until needed. You can even arrange to have funds held until a child enters college and then paid directly to the college itself.

In due course, you and your agent should design a method of payment properly suited to your needs. But here are a couple of points worth emphasizing:

(1) Don't set up too rigid a scheme. Between now and the time you die, things will change, and you might not remember later to change your insurance accordingly.

(2) If your beneficiaries are level-headed about money, let *them* have the option of deciding after your death how your insurance money should be paid. This you can do by leaving "All proceeds to [beneficiaries]. Proceeds to be held at interest, with the rights to withdraw all or part of the proceeds or to change to any other option reserved to the Beneficiaries."

(3) Unless you know that those who receive this money will have the very shrewdest of financial advice, the settlement options are the best bet that your family's funds will be safe and well handled.

BENEFICIARIES

Here again your agent may be very helpful. And yet, at least initially, he may not know enough about you, your family, and your estate to do more than make provisional arrangements. As a result, you may die leaving your policies all subject to a beneficiary clause worded something like this: "All Proceeds to Mary Smith, wife of the insured, if living; if not, then to the Children of this marriage equally, or to the survivors. If no issue, then to the Estate of the Insured." That's a fairly standard format, but it may not suit your particular needs at all. Suppose that either you or your wife has children by a previous marriage. As far as your insurance is concerned, this beneficiary arrangement leaves those children completely out in the cold.

On the subject of beneficiaries you should probably con-

233·

sult not only your agent but your lawyer as well. You do want to be sure that your life insurance fits neatly together with the rest of your estate so that both can be administered with the minimum of fuss. Furthermore, your lawyer may be able to find ways of minimizing or avoiding death-tax liabilities brought on by poorly arranged beneficiary devices. In short, like settlement options and the tricky question of who should own your life insurance, beneficiary arrangements should be put in the hands of experts.

REVIEWING YOUR INSURANCE

Once you and your agent have succeeded in putting your life insurance into proper shape, the need for periodic review is obvious. Some agents are thoughtful and businesslike enough to make semiannual or annual audits of their customers' policies. If you've got a good agent, he'll very likely make a special point of going over your insurance with you regularly. But unless you in turn make a habit of letting the agent know about changes in your situation, your policies will almost certainly become out of date. Thus, if a job promotion, an unexpected gift, or a break on the stock market suddenly transforms your financial life, you're foolish not to take the initiative and call in the insurance man. Likewise, if some economic disaster overtakes you, get your agent to help you cut back your insurance expenditures.

One other situation also deserves special mention here: what you should do if you must move and leave your agent behind. In the general rush of packing and moving, most people simply forget to notify the insurance agent. As a result, the following things often happen: (1) your life insurance policies get lost in the shuffle; (2) your premium notices don't follow you to your new location, so your policies lapse, at least temporarily; and (3) you end up in your new community without any sensible plan for taking care of your insurance needs.

If you let your agent know in advance that you will be moving, he can easily solve all these problems. For instance, he'll gladly hold your policies on file, and when things are untangled, send them on (having meanwhile notified the company or companies of your change of address). Moreover, he'll probably be able to recommend a good insurance man in your new home area; and—at your request—even make his own records available to his successor agent.

What Your Agent Won't Tell You

If the industry's promise of continuous lifetime service were really kept, your agent could always afford to be an objective advisor. But in life insurance, service almost always pivots on sales, which means that at some point you can count on having problems—and opportunities—that your agent cannot or will not help you handle. Indeed, it's already asking a good deal of this commission salesman to analyze and make necessary changes in policies you may have bought from someone else; hence the suggestion that you offer to pay him a fee. But in most cases not even a fee will buy you objectivity and service on some forms of life insurance, notably the group and savings-bank types. If you're interested in saving money on the insurance you do buy, you can't afford to overlook such "alien" insurance. Just don't expect much from your agent. With some justice, he believes that group insurance in particular is cutting his throat.

Group Insurance

Today group life insurance covers one out of every five Americans. With more than 180,000 employee groups enrolled, almost everyone who works for a company of any size has some group insurance. Your own employer probably has a group plan, and you very likely know that in most cases group life insurance is temporary (term) coverage, that the amount your firm offers you will depend on such factors as your earnings and your length of service, that the insurance stays in effect as long as you remain with your employer, and that group insurance can be converted into permanent insurance (by you) when you leave your job.

You may not know, however, that many employers are modernizing their group insurance programs by offering additional benefits. For instance, you yourself may be able to do any of the following:

(1) Buy with your own contributions more of this wholesale-rate insurance than your employer gives you free of charge.

(2) Take advantage of special superimposed group-insurance plans your firm may make available to executives or other employees.

(3) Use your own money to turn your group life insurance into special permanent coverage that will be completely paid up by the time you retire.

These are only a few examples of what's presently being done with group insurance. If you don't carefully scrutinize that mystifying brochure about your group coverage, you're missing a bet. For you may be able to pick up substantial additional insurance at nominal cost.

Indeed, if you own your own business, you may be even better off buying group insurance for all your employees—including, of course, yourself—than taking out additional insurance of your own. However, unlike individual policies, group-insurance contracts do vary widely in scope and cost; and therefore, you should shop around for group insurance. Your own agent may not be enough of a specialist to pick your group program. You should have him bring in experts to discuss the subject with you and your staff.

ASSOCIATION PLANS

If you belong to one of the professions—medicine, dentistry, law, accountancy, architecture—your national, state, and local professional associations all offer either group or quasi-group life insurance. These association plans do have their disadvantages (because the insurance is voluntary, the group may fill up with poor risks seeking non-medical coverage, and this anti-selection can drive up the rates). Nevertheless, the typical association plan offers a relatively cheap form of insurance. Your best strategy is to join whichever group seems to attract the younger members of your profession. For example, according to the reports, young doctors join their county and national associations rather than the state medical society.

Numerous other associations are now getting involved in group and quasi-group programs. Depending on the association, the plan may be good, not so good, or questionable in value. Don't join an association for insurance reasons only. If you do, so will others, and your group will be ruined as a low-cost-insurance medium. Unless the group is a healthy entity with its own reason for existing, you're going to end up with a very short-term insurance program.

TIAA–CREF

If you are a teacher, you may be eligible to participate in perhaps the finest of all private insurance programs, sponsored by the Carnegie Foundation and handled by the Teachers' Insurance and Annuity Association. The rates, products, and quality of TIAA are unmatched elsewhere.

And a superb retirement program is available to teachers and educational administrators through College Retirement Equities Fund, a TIAA affiliate specializing in variable annuities (see Chapter 9).

SAVINGS-BANK LIFE INSURANCE

In New York, Connecticut, and Massachusetts, many savings banks are licensed to sell life insurance over the counter. The advantage of savings-bank life insurance is simply that it's 15 to 20 per cent cheaper than what you buy from the insurance companies. So if saving money on insurance is one of your objectives and you're a resident of one of these three states, you'd do well to investigate such insurance.

Even though by current law (as influenced by the life insurance companies) the amount of savings-bank insurance you can own is limited, you will be required to pass a medical examination. Certain other legal restrictions make savings-bank policies slightly less flexible than those your agent sells you. But if your needs for insurance aren't overly complex, it makes good sense to side-step your agent—and become your own agent—in favor of savings-bank coverage.

GIMMICK POLICIES

By filling in your name, address, and age on the inside of a matchbook cover and mailing this "application" to a Midwestern insurance company, you can qualify for $1,000 worth of life insurance. The cost is usually about twice as much as you'd pay anywhere else legitimately. Similarly, you can buy life insurance by credit-card arrangement or you can order through the mail from a one-shot outfit located conveniently (for its owners) near the Canadian or Mexican borders.

As badly as the industry needs to modernize its distribution, these gimmick methods aren't much of a solution to either the industry's problems or your own. In general, the kinds of insurance that are sold by mail-order or other gimmicked-up methods have in common what one insurance man likes to call "post-mortem underwriting"; that is, you have to sue to collect. However picturesque, such lawsuits are both expensive and hard to win. Avoid the gimmicks, and save your heirs the trouble.

However, even the most reputable companies sometimes tolerate "special" arrangements that are actually no better than gimmicks. In recent years, for example, the biggest fad in life insurance has been the so-called "minimum deposit" way of buying a policy. Under minimum deposit you take out a large policy (for this purpose, many companies have designed special contracts that they sell only in amounts of $25,000 or more). Then from the insurance company or a bank (or even from the agent himself) you borrow enough money to pay all or part of each upcoming annual premium. Because the policy does possess cash value, the security for your loan can be the policy itself. And the policy is so designed that after a few years you can borrow each year's *entire* premium. This means that your only out-of-pocket expense is for the interest due on that steadily increasing loan. And since interest on loans is a deductible item for income-tax purposes, you supposedly realize a big saving in the cost of your life insurance.

However, minimum-deposit life insurance does pose certain other problems. For one thing, the higher the loan, the lower the death benefit, because when the borrower dies, the company recaptures the principal outstanding on the loan. (To counter this problem, some companies pile on extra term insurance that increases to cover the amount of the loan.) For another, each year's interest payments are

239·

higher than those of the year before, so that after a while you're spending more in interest than the original premium for the policy. Thus, for less and less insurance, you pay more and more money. After twenty years the whole process becomes hopelessly costly and futile.

To the discerning eye, minimum deposit looks suspiciously like an elaborate and very expensive version of term life insurance. Furthermore, the trickiness of the minimum-deposit system has a kind of sinister charm. But the real reason why billions of dollars' worth of this gimmicky coverage have been sold has nothing to do with tax savings. The fact is simply that if he can sell you minimum-deposit insurance, the agent makes a much higher commission than on a comparable amount of term insurance. For nearly a decade agents, with the help of the very same companies that publicly decry this "abuse" of the borrowing privilege, have been thumping the drum for minimum deposit. (Companies have even been formed specifically to merchandise minimum-deposit life insurance. And the industry has hired public relations men to plant articles in major magazines on the virtue of this borrow-now-pay-never scheme.)

Finally the Internal Revenue Service had to take action to cool off this gimmick. This they did by refusing to allow taxpayers full deduction of the loan interest. But the minimum-deposit scheme is still popular—too popular.

There's absolutely nothing illegal or immoral about borrowing on your insurance policies—or, for that matter, about surrendering them for their cash values. But it's stupid to borrow money to pay premiums (except in case of an emergency). The reason it's stupid is that the premiums are expensive enough, heaven knows, without throwing in interest charges on top of them. And if you're under the illusion that "you don't ever have to pay back" what you borrow from a life insurance company, just ask your beneficiaries what they think about those valueless pieces of paper you stick them with.

Eight Ways That Agents Can Cheat You

Despite your careful screening, the agent who passes your tests and eventually gains your confidence and your business may not be the man you thought he was. And in certain special situations (e.g., buying life insurance on a partner in your business or on a key employee), you may find yourself dealing with a stranger. So it makes sense to be alert to some of the common techniques insurance agents use to fatten their commissions at your expense, and to know about a few of the tricks they can play to persuade you that their policy is a real good deal.

(1) *The agent can lie about the premium.* This is a simple but almost foolproof method of getting you to spend more money on insurance. His ploy is to quote you a price accurate for a man a few years younger, then— when he delivers the policy—admit his "mistake." For $25 or $50 more a year, you'll probably go along (especially if the policy is a good-sized one).
The Answer. Unless you're convinced that his was an honest mistake (and errors in computation do happen), throw the bum out. Then get yourself an agent who doesn't make mistakes.

(2) *The agent can lie about dividends and cash values.* This makes the policy look considerably more attractive than it is, since if the dividends (on a mutual company's policy) are high, your premiums are lower; and if the cash values are richer, you get a better deal in case you surrender or borrow on the policy. Especially where the policy in question is a large one, the "sophisticated"

agent may be vague about dividends. The crooked agent is likely to falsify both sets of figures.

The Answer. Call the salesman's agency and ask to speak to the cashier. Read off the figures on the proposal the salesman has given you and ask for verification in writing over the *cashier's* signature (or that of the agency manager). You'd be surprised at how upset everybody will get if there's any discrepancy. If there is a gap between what the agent said and what his company tells you, do business elsewhere. And if you have time, turn the agent in to the state insurance department. They *might* decide to take away his license.

(3) *The agent can try to sell you a policy altogether different from the one you wanted.* This stratagem is considered smart business by many agents and their managers. It's the insurance equivalent of "trading you up," as practiced by other kinds of businesses. The agent may tell you that the alternate policy he brings back to you is better. What he really means is that it's bigger or costlier or both.

The Answer. Throw the bum out. Life insurance isn't a car or a TV set. You can't afford to fool around with smooth merchandisers.

(4) *The agent may try to sell you a related product,* or what he tells you is a related product—shares in a mutual fund, for instance, or some form of medical insurance. He's hoping that because you're in the mood to take out life insurance, you'll also sign up for something extra. Customers have been known to make "impulse purchases" of mutual funds, disability-insurance policies, and the like at a price exceeding the original life insurance premium.

The Answer. Unless you have specifically asked for the related product, have nothing to do with such "collateral" offers. Buy your stocks and bonds or mutual funds from a broker or specialist. Keep your disability insurance (and your medical insurance) for another day, and do only what you set out to do.

(5) *The agent or his company can do you a favor if you become a customer.* Need money? The agent will arrange a loan. Looking for a new house? The agent can fix you up. Very versatile man, your agent. But as a "courtesy," you have to buy the insurance—and perhaps even take out a bigger policy than you wanted. For instance, the agent tells you that he can get his company to refinance your mortgage on highly favorable terms. You *do* need insurance to cover that mortgage in case you die before it's paid off. He's got just the policy. So sign the application for insurance and the papers for the mortgage deal, and he'll reduce your monthly mortgage payments, get you some cash from the company (for the difference between the old mortgage and the new), and even prepay the insurance premiums. Sound good? Well, don't forget that you're putting your house in hock all over again, paying new legal fees, new title fees, and all the rest, including what may be higher interest. You might also keep in mind that the agent's only doing this for commission on the life insurance that he sells. Only in the hands of the most upright and honorable agent can this plan work to your advantage. *The Answer.* NO. Go to your bank for refinancing mortgages—and to some other agent for life insurance.

(6) *The agent can offer you a rebate*—some or all of his commission—to get you to buy insurance. He keeps the renewal commissions, and you pay only half the first year's premium.

The Answer. He's a crook if he makes the offer, and you're a crook if you accept it. In most states rebating is a criminal offense. If either one of you is caught, you face a fine or even a jail term—and it serves you right. If you can't afford the insurance, buy what you can afford or forget it.

(7) *The agent can conceal the fact that for health or other reasons you're being charged extra.* In order to make the sale, he may even pay the extra premium himself—and

leave you to find out about the rated-up policy when the next premium falls due.

The Answer. Make the agent explain that policy page by page. If you see any such phrase as Special Class I, or Substandard Class IV, demand a full explanation. Then get rid of the agent.

(8) *The agent can try to make you give up your old policy or policies for the cash to buy his big new one.* Such "twisting" is looked upon with pious horror by all agents and companies when their own policy owners are the ones who are fast-talked into surrendering existing policies. Every agent in the business runs across situations where the replacement of old insurance seems advantageous. But most agents aren't trained well enough to analyze the pros and cons of a given situation. They earn commissions only if they sell new insurance; hence, "twisting" is widespread.

The Answer. If the agent suggests that you surrender or borrow on old policies in order to buy new insurance, demand a detailed statement in writing of the advantages *and disadvantages* of the move. (There are *always* some disadvantages.) Then work out what you're giving up and what you're getting. In general, you're better off buying a smaller amount of new insurance and keeping the old than dropping policies bought when you were younger and the cost was lower. That "great new policy" the agent wants to sell you will almost certainly cost you more than those old policies do.

DEATH CLAIMS

When, in the final marvelous euphemism of the trade, a policy "matures" as a death claim, several things happen. We assume that your family has notified your company or companies as quickly as possible. The company in turn springs into action with unwonted efficiency. Within a very few days the company puts into your beneficiaries' hands the death-claims forms, brief statements to be completed, signed, and returned along with (1) the attending physician's report of the cause and date of death, (2) a certified copy of the Death Certificate, and (3) the policy or policies themselves. Only then does your policy really mature.

The next step depends on the nature of the arrangements for settling the estate. If you had made no settlement-option provisions, the company will sometimes suggest to your beneficiaries the use of those options. (Most companies do this.) If your beneficiaries still elect to have the money paid in one lump sum, the company either mails the check or has an agent deliver it. Where the beneficiaries decide to use the settlement options instead, the company sends or has delivered a so-called "supplementary contract," spelling out the details of the settlement. At the same time, any initial payment under the chosen arrangement is made.

Here, obviously, a capable agent could be a godsend. It's part of his job to do all the paper work of death: to collect all the policies, to obtain the necessary forms and process them, to ask the right questions and make the right suggestions to your family. He'll also know how to get action out of your firm's Insurance Department, how to contact the Veterans' Administration (for G.I. insurance) and the Social Security Administration. And when his immediate task is over, the decent agent will know how to fade unobtrusively into the background where he belongs.

Some Do's And Don'ts

If you keep your life insurance policies and related documents together in a single, known place, you make life easier for yourself and for your beneficiaries. Surprisingly, however, your safe-deposit box is the *worst* place to leave such vital papers. Once you're dead, the bank must seal that box, which can then be opened only in the presence of an auditor from the state tax authorities. This may mean considerable delay at just the wrong time; so you are better off keeping those policies at home in a desk drawer.

If you have any special wishes or requirements to transmit to your beneficiaries about the use of your life insurance, leave specific written instructions, rather than vague verbal hints. But the most important thing of all is simply not to *worry* about life insurance. Indeed, the suggestions in this chapter are designed to spare you from the need to wonder whether you've planned wisely and "done the right thing."

The next step, and almost the last, is to pay special attention to the final users of most life insurance, the wives, who may someday be dealing with your policies and the money they provide.

> "Don't worry, dear. Ben will take care of everything."
>
> *—a husband to his wife*

11 . *Women, Wives, and Widows:*
Insurance for the Ladies

"IT'S BLOOD MONEY. I don't want one penny of blood money on my conscience." This was the strange excuse one young woman gave an agent for refusing to let her husband buy life insurance. Only by arranging a surreptitious meeting at the agent's office could the husband actually make the purchase, and thenceforth he had to lie to his wife about the reason for spending the premium money.

This is an extreme case of what insurance salesmen call the Wife Problem. Today such superstitiousness about "blood money" has almost vanished. According to the surveys, wives strongly believe that their husbands *should* carry life insurance, especially if there are small children in the family. Furthermore, wives are now supposed to be "realistic" about the possibility of a husband's premature death, and most women are quite aware that they're likely to outlive men the same age by at least six or seven years. Radio and television shows, magazine articles, lectures, and "clinics" now offer women all kinds of advice about investments and finance, including the matter of how to handle their husbands' estate. Since its publication in 1956, a book called *Teach Your Wife to Be a Widow*—perhaps the ultimate in how-to literature—has sold handsomely.

This frankness seems like a refreshing change from Victorian taboos about discussing death, and particularly the business side of death, with one's wife. Such openness also mirrors the shift in the social and economic status of women, who can now expect to share equally with men the details and headaches of managing money. And yet, despite all the lectures and books, the Wife Problem—and the entire question of what women should know and do about life insurance—is still a puzzle. The insurance industry, inarticulate enough in talking to people in general, is absolutely tongue-tied when it comes to dealing with women. Partly because of this, and partly because many women feel uneasy and tongue-tied themselves about what is still a delicate subject, to the fair sex life insurance is a vaguely unpleasant mystery —and a bore. As a leading agent puts it, "The single gal couldn't care less, the married woman lets her husband take care of the insurance, and the widow finds out too late."

So this chapter is designed especially for readers who check *F* instead of *M* on questionnaires—for every woman, whether single or married.

As a wife and mother, the woman who reads these pages may one day *have* to know something about life insurance. Each year, some 600,000 newly widowed women must contend with their husbands' insurance. And each year, as beneficiaries, widows and their children share well over $2,000,000,000 worth of insurance death benefits. Because there is always a chance, however remote, that she will suddenly join these ranks, insurance is something that every married woman needs to understand.

Even before we come to the matter of being well informed

about your husband's insurance, we should consider another set of problems which, as a woman who owns or is thinking of buying life insurance, you may find disturbing. About 60 per cent of the women of working age do own some—but not very much—insurance (the average amount is under $2,000 worth). Much of this insurance is not consciously purchased, but automatically provided (the group insurance that comes with the job, for example, or the small policy that your parents took out for you when you were a child). This means that while many women are insured, the *specific insurance needs of women* are rarely considered.

Do Women Need Life Insurance?

Some do, some don't. Ironically, many women who need life insurance don't have any, while millions of women who wouldn't—and shouldn't—think of buying insurance are insured. Many young mothers, whose premature deaths could cause serious financial problems, go without life insurance because the family budget just won't stretch that far. Yet a great many young working women with no economic dependents and thus no need for insurance are automatically covered by group-insurance programs. This is one more sample of the profound illogic behind today's methods of marketing insurance.

But whether or not you yourself need to carry life insurance can't be answered by quoting statistics or uttering generalities. Like your brothers, husband, and male friends, you should base your insurance plans on your own private thoughts about life, death, and money. Those thoughts in turn depend on who you are and what you are.

A sensitive woman, one of the approximately 25,000 female insurance agents, commented, "Most women fear old age, illness, loneliness, and deprivation of love more than they fear death itself."

That may well be true. Perhaps the only thing a man can add is that life insurance is no real solution to the problems that everyone must face as he grows older. Just as it's not a magic talisman that protects its owner from ever dying, so too is an insurance policy no protection against life.

Too many women buy life insurance because "it's a good way to save for old age" or "my father believes in life insurance." But in thinking about insurance, be more specific with yourself than that. There are easier (and probably more profitable) ways to save money than by means of a life insurance policy—by making contributions to your company's pension plan, by having your bank siphon some of your salary into a savings account, or simply by going to the savings bank faithfully yourself. And what makes great sense for a father may be completely impractical for his daughter.

So when you ponder what your death could mean to others, you may decide that at this point you feel no financial obligation to those who will survive you. If that's the case, you truly need no insurance, and whatever life insurance you may be carrying is superfluous, at least for the time being. On the other hand, you may discover that you feel strongly about leaving money to provide for a child's well-being, to help support an aging parent, or to answer some other need. Then, and only then, does it make sense for you to consider buying insurance on your life.

INSURANCE AND THE WORKING GIRL

You may be a young girl just starting her first job, with no dependents, and marriage only a distant dream. Under these circumstances, the insurance that comes with your job may be more an inconvenience than anything else, but what do you do about that insurance? Or you may be married, a mother, and still working because you enjoy it and because your family can use the extra income. In your situation, what part, if any, should life insurance play? To pick still another example, you may be in your late thirties or over forty, unmarried, working hard at your career. Do you own any life insurance? Is your insurance the right kind and amount for your needs? Anyway, what are those needs?

For the woman who works, getting information about life insurance isn't too difficult. If you have questions about your group insurance, there's always the lady in the Personnel Department who looks after employee benefits, or there's your supervisor or the boss. Even if nobody in your office is an expert, you do have a bank whose officers will either give you advice or steer you to someone who can help. And in case you don't want or can't get personal counseling, you can always write to the insurance company's Customer Service Department. (Of course, the letter you'll get back will probably be twice as confusing as your policy itself, so this is something of a desperate remedy.)

As a woman, moreover, you have certain privileges. Without embarrassment, you can insist on clear explanations and ask naïve questions. Unlike a man, you won't be tempted to pretend that you know all about insurance when you really don't. Because you're not as obvious a target as a man (and because nothing is more sacred to a life insurance agent than the ideal of American Womanhood), you'll very likely get more courteous and lower-pressure treatment than the unfortunate male ever gets. At small cost in time and energy, you can wind up better informed about life insurance than most men are. Your biggest problem will be that insurance experts aren't used to thinking about women as *customers*. As a result, their suggestions are likely to be unimaginative and dull.

251 ·

Let's go back to the examples mentioned earlier to see if there aren't some ways to enliven your own interest and set you thinking a bit differently about insurance. Even if you are a single girl carrying insurance you don't really need, your policy or group certificate can still serve a useful function. First, be sure you understand its details. Then, as beneficiary of your insurance, why not name your college or church or a charity in which you are interested? If the unlikely were to happen, if you suddenly died, those few thousands of dollars would then have a valid purpose—a purpose perhaps more meaningful than you'd gain by leaving the money to parents or other relatives.

If you're an older woman, not married, the security of a life insurance policy may seem tempting. You may rightly feel that it's up to you to set aside money for retirement; and special forms of insurance called "endowment" or "retirement income" policies offer automatic ways of saving for that future need. However, as noted earlier, there are alternative ways of accumulating money, ways that don't involve your carrying life insurance when you might not need it. Even if the policy offers what seems to be a good-sized profit, paying you considerably more than you put in over the years, remember that time and compound interest make any savings program profitable. Investigate those alternatives and don't buy a retirement policy involving life insurance unless you want to leave money to someone should you die *before* retirement.

If you are nearing retirement now, you may want to consider buying an annuity. Here too, however, your decision should be based on your own situation and needs. Most life insurance agents know next to nothing about annuities, only that they guarantee a regular fixed income to the owner for as long as she lives. But special forms offer other guarantees as well (for instance, that if the owner dies within a stated

period of time, the payments will continue to another beneficiary for a prearranged number of years). Furthermore, not
only insurance companies but colleges and other institutions
(the Salvation Army is the best known but not necessarily
the most liberal) make annuities available. The tax advantages of these "charitable annuities" are seldom mentioned
by insurance agents, because the agent wants you to buy his
product instead. If you write to your college or to a favorite
charity, you'll undoubtedly receive an interested response.
But you should definitely consult a lawyer before making
charitable annuity arrangements.

Marriage

The life insurance industry assures the American male
that on the day his bride walks down the aisle, his financial
responsibilities and his need for life insurance become
urgent. In some cases this is still true. Many wives do quit
their jobs to take up housekeeping immediately after getting
married, and many husbands must therefore accept total
responsibility for family support at once. But many more
women continue to work after marriage, and sometimes they
even bring home the bulk of the new family's bacon. How
urgent is the husband's need for life insurance in this situation? And more to the immediate point, what about "wife
insurance"?

Although there are no ready answers, it's no longer a
truism that your husband *must* buy insurance or *more* insurance the minute he slips the gold band on your finger.
On the contrary, it may make good sense for a newly wed
couple to wait six months or longer before choosing a life
insurance agent and taking out insurance. You and your
husband will undoubtedly have other expenses to meet,
budgets to establish, and so forth. Don't forget completely

about life insurance, but don't be in haste to buy it either.

If both you and your husband are working, his real need for insurance doesn't arise until you leave your job to have children. He may wish to anticipate that need by buying life insurance in advance. But as long as you're more or less self-supporting, his requirements are probably modest. You can help by keeping *his* sales resistance high (since he's going to be the target for solicitations) and by knowing enough about insurance to discuss the matter intelligently. Thus, you might ask yourself whether you would need the extra money if he were to die.

As far as insurance on your life is concerned, it all depends. You may be putting your husband through law or medical school or working to let him complete his Ph.D. The normal situation is reversed and temporarily you are the breadwinner. If your premature death could wreck your husband's career, you might be very wise to consider insuring your own life and *not* your husband's. Here temporary term insurance makes the best sense—the insurance remaining in effect until your husband finishes his studies and begins to earn money.

But unless you have such a special reason for buying, put life insurance at the very bottom of your expense list and use the money for more fruitful purchases. However, don't forget to make the necessary changes—new address, your husband as beneficiary—in any insurance you already own and plan to keep.

Children

Both you and your husband will undoubtedly feel that having children makes life insurance on his life almost mandatory. If you haven't done so already, you'll now go through the process of choosing an agent and taking out insurance.

You owe it to yourself and your youngsters not to disappear into the kitchen or bedroom during the interviews between your husband and the agent. And you certainly should take note of the agent's recommendations and of what your husband actually buys. Now is obviously the time to do some thinking and talking about premature death. Even if you're appalled at the idea and don't want to discuss it, you should at least know what your husband's thoughts and plans are. Make him explain those plans, for you're the one who will have to carry them out.

During one of the selling interviews the insurance man may go to work on your husband about *you*. "Bill, do you carry insurance on Ann's life?"

"No, we've never thought of it."

"Well, have you ever thought about all the things a wife does for her family? She cooks, cleans, keeps house, chauffeurs the kids around, entertains your guests, and a thousand and one other things besides. You only have to do one job, but your wife has many different jobs.

"If anything happened to Ann, you'd have to hire not one but several full-time employees to do all those things she does for you and the kids. Wouldn't you, Bill?"

"Well, I—"

"So don't you think," the agent goes on relentlessly, "that you should carry at least some insurance on Ann's life? To have enough money to replace her services in case, God forbid, something does happen?"

You may heartily agree with the agent that if you weren't around, your husband would be in the soup. Just to add up the cost of your domestic toil as cook, charwoman, nursemaid, laundress, gardener, and hostess is enough to make your head spin. And so, you may be grateful that someone, even if only the insurance man, points out and appreciates your special contribution to the family economy. But before you urge your husband to buy insurance on you, take a deep breath.

Unfortunately, the agent's logic doesn't stand up under everyday reality.

Just as your husband's life insurance can never be more than a terribly inadequate substitute for his own earning power (see Chapter 10) so must insurance on your life fall far short of replacing the value of your services to *him*. Let's be honest. Your death would mean the total rearrangement of your family's life, and the few thousand dollars' worth of insurance that the agent is trying so hard to sell won't really make that much difference. On the contrary, by giving you and your husband a totally false sense of security ("We've solved the problem with wife insurance"), the insurance man may be doing you a disservice.

Your real security comes from facing the possibility that you might die young, from planning with your husband for even this disaster, and from being the kind of woman whose family is a kind of small miracle of strength. No insurance man can supply that security ready-made, and $5,000 or $10,000 worth of life insurance, bought on impulse because the agent scares you, is a wretched alternative.

Only if your death would add financial catastrophe to your family's grief, should you let your husband buy the insurance. The odds against your dying young are very remote, while the chances are excellent that you and your husband can use the premium money for more immediate purposes.

Divorce

Among the many things that become grist for the lawyers in a divorce, your husband's life insurance may be prominent. You and your attorney will probably feel that under the separation agreement, your husband should carry life insurance in favor of you and the children. For you, such insurance may only be one of the drearier details, while to your husband the expense may be burdensome. If your parting is at all amicable, there are special arrangements that help solve his problem and thus guarantee that adequate insurance will be part of the settlement. For instance, your lawyers should explore the idea of joint ownership of the policy. This means that your husband keeps control of the cash equity in his insurance, while you and the children retain an irrevocable interest in the death benefits. Under such an arrangement both parties are better off, and a husband can often (for technical reasons) afford to carry more insurance.

If you are granted custody of your children, you may wish to carry life insurance on your own life. You may even want your husband to take care of the premiums. When you buy the insurance, however, make sure that as beneficiaries, your children are represented by a legal guardian. Otherwise, if you die while the children are still minors, the insurance company will delay payment until the court appoints someone as guardian. Simply by checking with your lawyer, you can avoid any such problem entirely.

How to Be a Good Beneficiary

The crux of a woman's involvement with life insurance is that she may have to cope with policies and proceeds after her husband's death. One thing goes without saying. What you know and do today about your husband's life insurance can make a vast difference if your husband dies too soon. You may already be versed in his financial affairs. Whenever your husband discusses insurance or sits down with his agent to buy more, you may make a point of being alertly present. You and your husband may have gone over in detail his will, his estate, and other blueprints for a future without him.

But the chances are you haven't.

You probably have a sketchy knowledge of your family's finances. You may have, for instance, a fair idea of what your house is worth and some notion of how much life insurance your husband carries. But do you know much more? There may be a great deal to know. Perhaps your husband wants to spare you the need to understand such complex and disturbing matters as the plans for his estate. "My husband's told me again and again," one woman said proudly, "that if anything happens to him, all I have to do is call Ben. 'Ben will take care of everything.' That's what he says." Ben is the family lawyer, and in this case it's true that the lady's husband has left complete, detailed instructions and enough money to guarantee that his instructions will be carried out.

Even so, the husband is missing a bet. He's thought of everything *except* explaining things to his wife and thus reassuring her that everything *is* taken care of. For you, as for her, certain questions should be answered and certain details made crystal clear. Let's list some of those details:

(1) Where does your husband keep his insurance policies and other important documents? If you don't know, find out and make a note of the location.

(2) Within $1,000 either way, you should know how much insurance your husband is carrying. You should also know the names and home-office addresses of the insurance companies in question. Along with your insurance man's name and address, you should jot down this additional information and keep it available.

(3) You may well want to know whether your husband's in-

surance is payable to you directly, to your children, or to his estate. In short, who's the beneficiary?

(4) Aside from life insurance, do you have any source of ready money in the emergency situation of your husband's death?

(5) Whom has your husband chosen to look after things in case of that emergency? Is there a family lawyer or other advisor? Do you know the man and trust him?

This is by no means everything. But unless you are absolutely certain about the above basic facts, don't attempt to know more. Instead, pursue your husband until he gives you this information. This much you have the right, not to mention the obligation, to understand.

Beyond these basics, there are dozens of other facts that in your particular situation may be essential. For instance, is your husband covered under Social Security? If so, what's his Social Security number? What insurance company handles his group insurance at the office? Does his company have a pension or profit-sharing plan? Who can give you accurate information about such benefits? If your husband is in business for himself, is there someone—a partner, lawyer, or accountant—who knows and can explain to you the details of the business?

You'll naturally have your own questions, and you should make up a list and ask them. Your husband may be evasive or even resentful if you act like an inquisitor, so ask your questions a few at a time. Obviously, you're in search of information, not trying to remake your husband's financial arrangements. Even if those arrangements seem to you inadequate, it's one thing to find out where you stand and another to convey to your spouse that you are panicky. After all, your husband is very much alive, which means that you will have time to correct any serious weakness in his plans.

DEATH

Chapter 10 covers the inevitable, grim paper work of death. Perhaps the most important point to add here is that you need expert, trustworthy advisors when it comes to the proper handling of an estate. Well-meaning friends and relatives may be at a loss. Worse, they may infect you with their own dismay. So even if you are left with what seems like very little money, be prepared to seek—and take—the advice of a really good lawyer, one who specializes in estate and trust law. To help you handle immediate or routine money problems, get hold of an officer of your bank. Along with these specialists, listen to your insurance man's ideas. (Wherever possible, have the insurance man and the lawyer work together and confer with you together.)

Unless you're faced with a financial as well as a personal crisis, don't make *any* money decision in haste. Don't hurry to put your home on the market; don't sell those shares of stock you find in the safe-deposit box; don't drastically cut back your standard of living. The longer you can defer such plans, the more time you can give yourself, the better. The bank, the stockbroker, or the insurance company can wait if you can. Therefore, take your time.

INSURANCE ON CHILDREN

In a kind of automatic, conditioned social reflex, many families take out small policies on each child at birth (or shortly after). Such "juvenile policies" are designed to mature at age twenty-one, when the cash equity is worth a thousand, or several thousand, dollars. The agent rarely has much trouble convincing parents that this modest pot of gold that will give your son "a start in life" or your daughter a dowry has special, magical virtues. One popular variant of the juvenile policy is the "jumping juvenile," which provides that when the youngster reaches twenty-one, his $1,000 worth of insurance will suddenly blossom into $5,000 worth.

If there is such a thing as an impulse purchase in life insurance, a policy on a small child is precisely that. In most cases juvenile insurance is absolutely pointless. You're not *completely* wasting the money you spend insuring your youngsters (because juvenile policies do offer savings features), but you are tying up money unnecessarily, and if you cancel or lapse the policy, some of your dollars will be lost.

Even the agent will concede that insurance on a child's life serves no real economic purpose. It doesn't replace a lost earning power, and it's not the bargain that the salesman may call it. Contrary to popular belief, juvenile-insurance premiums aren't very much lower than adult rates. At zero, four, fourteen, or twenty-four, the total outlay for insurance is about the same.

But the most important reason for not buying juvenile insurance is that (especially among families most charmed by the idea) the premiums would be better spent on insurance for the breadwinner.

Unless you have a special reason (like a complicated trust fund where insurance is essential), be unsentimental when the agent starts his sales pitch. Let your kids grow up with savings in the bank instead of insurance, and don't be your own child's beneficiary.

The Last Word

Life insurance isn't blood money. As one agent observed (and not cynically either), "I've never yet heard of a widow who turned down an insurance check." But neither is insurance the magical guarantee of security for wives and children that the ads, the agents, and the industry make it out to be. Yet the industry expects you to believe, without any real understanding, in the magical virtues of life insurance. If any group of Americans has the right to feel simultaneously used and neglected by this industry, that group is our womenfolk.

On the surface, the life insurance people are almost the only businessmen left in America who don't use sex to sell their product. (Today even the banks are trying out pretty models in ads.) As insensitive as they are about advertising and public relations, insurance men aren't foolish enough to think that a blonde in a bikini will automatically improve *their* sales. But though you're not supposed to be sexy, you are nevertheless the insurance industry's chief merchandising tool. If you want to know what this industry really thinks about you, take a look at the women in their ads—simpering matrons with that hubby-wifey-folksy look and a couple of freckled kids in the background.

To get your husbands, the daddies of America, to pour more money into their industry, insurance men rely on fictions about women far more unreal and far more degrading than the image of the girl in the bikini. For instance, as part of their training, insurance salesmen have drummed into their heads that "women can't handle money," that "in an emergency, the average woman won't know what to do or where to turn for help." The salesman is taught to suggest to your husband that you're a dear, good girl who must at all costs—and it costs plenty—be sheltered from life. And death.

In an era when every other consumer industry bends over backward to appeal to women, this heavy-handed Victorianism is startling and depressing. Simply from your trips to the store, you know that today's marketing experts see women, not men, as America's best, shrewdest customers. Why else would a leading manufacturer of hand tools package a special set, including a hammer, a saw, screwdrivers, pliers, just for women? At the other end of the scale, Detroit's automobile-makers have built their postwar empires on what they've learned about you and your needs. Not only the pastel colors and carpeted floors of your car, but its power steering and brakes—not only the frills, but the essentials as well—are designed specifically for you. Indeed, you are Big Business.

Insurance men know perfectly well that millions of American women work, earn money, and spend it. (They should know, for two thirds of their industry's own employees are women, though except in "service" departments like Personnel there are almost no female life insurance executives.) The industry's top brass is aware that either alone or with your husband, you make most of the family's important buying decisions. Despite what they know, the men who run life insurance still won't wake up to reality and treat you with the respect you deserve. That's what a century of parochialism and ingrained conservatism has done to this industry.

They'll be polite to you and exploit their lace-doily image, but the men who convince your husband to buy insurance don't really think you're important. You're the Wife Problem, at first an obstacle in the salesman's path and finally, perhaps, the recipient of a form letter like the one that follows:

Dear Mrs.——: We deeply regret to learn of the death of your husband (brother, father) who was covered under Policy(ies) # ——. Enclosed is our check for $——, made out to you as Beneficiary. You will no doubt want to know how this figure was arrived at. A calculation sheet showing that information is attached. If you have any questions, please consult our Customer Service Department.

To the final user of its product, the American life insurance industry has nothing more than this to say.

Epilogue

AND SO, WE'RE STUCK with the life insurance industry, not to mention all that insurance.

As a private business, the industry is run by a few men at the top, who are in the insurance game mostly for what they can get out of it—money, power, and prestige. As a public institution, the industry falls far short of telling the truth and keeping its promises, either to the people who do its work or to the public that supports it. And as the only place we can go to get insurance, the industry is limited in its aims and monopolistic in many of its practices. Thus, some of us are heavily overpersuaded and oversold, while others seldom or never have the chance to own insurance. And all of us pay too much money for the insurance we do buy.

Nothing in this indictment of the industry is new.

Ever since the American life insurance industry began a hundred and fifty years ago, critics of life insurance have been saying such things. In every generation there have been insurance scandals, exposures, hearings, government inquiries, and then new laws and supposed reforms. But the growth of the industry has continued unchecked, to the point

265·

where we can't even measure its power and influence, let alone control its growth.

In our society life insurance obviously isn't the only institution that has gotten, or seems to be getting, out of hand. Growth has overtaken almost every institution, from the grocery store to the federal government. We accept the fact of growth simply because we must. As a society, we are good at making things more efficient as we make them bigger. But growth without change is one thing a society like ours shouldn't accept. What disfigures the insurance industry most is precisely this mindless growth—in wealth, in power, in importance—without change.

That life insurance is losing ground in a few areas (notably its share of our savings dollars) may mean that the American public is changing its attitude toward insurance. As long as we are prostrate before this giant, there's little hope that any organized effort can contain or control it.

Yet as an individual, you can do something.

You can't prevent the industry from hiring as agents hundreds of thousands of men who will fail.

But you can find yourself a decent, sympathetic man to handle your own life insurance. And the next time your telephone rings and some stranger asks for an appointment "just to go over your policies" you can say "No."

You can't keep the industry's investment wizards from using the policy owners' money to make dubious investments.

But you can refuse to do business with an agent who offers to "get you a good deal" on your mortgage if you'll buy his policy.

You can't keep the industry's biggest companies from holding hands with the state regulatory bodies that are meant to supervise life insurance.

But you can turn over a crooked agent to the law.

You can't get this industry to lower its rates.

But you can make sure that you only buy insurance to cover your family's real needs and that you don't waste a nickel on extras.

Finally, you can't change a society that wants *not* to wonder about life insurance and *not* to see how bizarre, how really strange, is our obsession with insurance.

But you can be aware that other things matter a lot more than life insurance.

About the Author

James Gollin learned the insurance business from the inside. During eight years as an agent for one of the largest companies in the industry, he sold enough insurance to win six Field Club awards, and in several of those years he sold more than $500,000 worth of insurance. He also earned the degree of Chartered Life Underwriter and has been a member of the National Association of Life Underwriters.

Born in St. Louis, Missouri, Mr. Gollin grew up in Scarsdale, New York. Although he received an A.B. and an M.A. in English from Yale University, he turned to writing professionally only after extensive experience in retailing, advertising, and insurance. The author, his wife, and their two sons live in Manhattan, in an apartment filled with books, art, and a collection of early musical instruments including a homemade harpsichord. Since 1963 Mr. Gollin has devoted much of his time to the research, interviewing, and analysis for *Pay Now, Die Later*.